NERVOUS CHRISTIANS

By
L. Gilbert Little, M.D.

Concluding Chapter By
Theodore H. Epp

SCHOOL OF TOMORROW®

Lewisville, Texas

Reprinted but not edited by School of Tomorrow®
2600 Ace Lane
P.O. Box 299000
Lewisville, Texas 75029-9000

ISBN 1-56265-057-2

1 2 3 4   Printing/Year   99 98 97 96

FOREWORD

L. Gilbert Little, M.D., received his degree from the University of Arkansas and is a member of the American Psychiatric Association and of the American Medical Association. He has had twenty-five years of psychiatric experience, three and one-half of which he spent as physician in charge of Hawthornden State Hospital, in Ohio He has a strong Christian testimony, is active in the Christian Business Men's Committee, and is a member of the board of directors of Grace Bible Institute, of Omaha, Nebraska. His present practice is in Wichita, Kansas.

Dr. Little's contribution to this book covers an area of counseling that may come as a surprise to many Christian workers, for the tendency these days is to think that in academic psychology and psychiatry lies the key to the problems that beset all of us, in some degree or another. The method which Dr. Little follows is found in the Bible itself. Those responding to it have found happy deliverance from present-day tensions and strains.

Theodore H. Epp, founder and director of the Back to the Bible Broadcast, has added a chapter dealing with a cause of mental and emotional disturbances of which many Christians are ignorant. As does Dr. Little, he points the child of God to Christ's work on Calvary as the means of victory.

Not all believers belong in the category of the "nervous" Christian, but none of us will read these pages without recognizing some things familiar to our own experiences. After having read this book, we should understand ourselves better, have greater compassion for those around us, and thank God with deeper gratitude for salvation in Christ.

—John I. Paton

CONTENTS

1

CAN PSYCHIATRY
SOLVE SOUL PROBLEMS?

An elderly patient once said to me, "Doctor, can we change our thinking when we are old? Can psychiatry change us?"

Psychiatry always finds this a very perplexing question. Not only is it perplexing, but in Christian psychotherapy it is pathetic, because the question almost always comes from an unregenerated heart, which apparently can no longer derive pleasure from "the lust of the flesh, and the lust of the eyes, and the pride of life" (I John 2:16).

This is an age-old question. Nicodemus, a ruler of the Jews, a man of learning and power, asked the Lord Jesus how a man could change when he is old. Jesus answered him, "That which is born of the flesh is flesh; and that which is born of the Spirit is spirit" (John 3:6). In the light of his fleshly nature he could not understand the things of the Spirit, because "they are spiritually discerned." "But the natural man receiveth not the things of the Spirit of God: for they are foolishness unto him" (I Cor. 2:14).

The natural, unregenerate man cannot change his thinking, because his thinking is unspiritual; and unspiritual people can think only of self. When

5

we look about us and see the highway of the natural man strewn with neurotic wrecks who cannot change their thinking by their own power, it is apparent that the flesh-nature is not able to find peace through the lusts of the flesh. Being devoid of the indwelling Holy Spirit, the self-nature is a ready prey for satanic culture.

Emotional Sickness—So-Called Nervousness

Thousands upon thousands of patients have emotional conflicts because they cannot make a satisfactory adjustment to the world. They make up the 60 to 75 per cent of the patients who show up in doctors' offices and receive the diagnosis, "There is nothing wrong physically. You are just nervous." They are seeking help—release from the satanic bondage of fear, anxiety, and worry.

Enslavement is never sudden; it is a subtle beguilement, taking in the individual's whole lifetime. Can patients tear themselves loose from satanic bondage after their meditations have been a lifetime forming a habit pattern? Being in fellowship with Satan, they have learned to look to him and his worldly pleasures and achievements for satisfaction in this life to divert the anxious mind from worry.

A worldly businessman, bent on achieving success in accumulating much of this world's goods, set up a goal for himself, turning all his thoughts and meditations to his own ambition in life, until he had no other interest but self. He lived in constant fear and anxiety that his business venture might collapse. He developed various gastric disturbances which had no organic basis, and his physicians advised, "You must get away from your work."

He followed a rather typical course, characteristic of "nervous" patients, trying various medicines, hoping to get relief for his gastric distress and his varied bodily tensions. These symptoms made him fearful, and he questioned himself, "What if these symptoms would become so severe that doctors could not help me?" He tried hospital rest, sedatives, shots, and short and long vacations, which only worried him because he was away from his business—his love.

This patient sought psychiatry, expecting relief from his distressing symptoms, but psychiatry could give him only temporary relief; it could not cure. For such patients there is only one cure. When they accept Jesus Christ as their Saviour and believe in the finished work of Christ on the cross of Calvary, they have peace in their souls. When there is peace in the soul, there is no fear, no anxiety, no worry.

Many psychiatric patients, like the businessman, may make a physical and mental recovery; yet the vexation in the soul remains to come forth periodically to torture the mind with doubts, anxieties, fears, and bodily tensions.

Satanic Bondage

Christ leads His sheep; when they follow Him, there can be no anxiety, fear, or worry. But Satan drives his slaves, energizing them with fear and anxiety. The constant worry. (nervousness) drives them to seek rest somewhere, somehow. Satan offers countless diversions that make their appeal to the lust of the flesh through sensual sin, which is no longer considered sin since he has modernized the terminology of sins. For example, sodomy has become homosexuality; adultery has been changed to free love; the drunkard is a respected alcoholic; and the murderer is temporarily insane. Furthermore, Satan is successfully indoctrinating the world to believe that sin is no longer sin by using apostate teachers, whom he ensnares for his purposes (Tit. 1:16).

The "prince of the power of the air" is ever on the alert to block any soul that might be tempted to raise a cry to God for deliverance, by quickly coming to his own with a new remedy for "nerves" and suggesting diabolical diversions. But these do not change the thinking pattern; they merely divert the thoughts for the time being. They do not relieve the patient of fear, because "fear hath torment" (I John 4:18).

Things of the Flesh Do It

Reason and experience tell the unregenerate to change his thoughts by accepting an appeasement through the avenue of "the lust of the eyes," encouraging the careworn to gaze on the screen and bask on a lustful life, which he does not have a license to live out in actual life. Indulging in fantastic sensuality affords temporary diversion for millions.

Knowledge, success, and power in this present world do not change heart meditations. These feed the self (ego) with a personal satisfaction that "I myself" have accomplished something. Many unregenerate souls are carried through this present world by the energizing power, "the pride of life."

In order to prevent disappointments and frustrations many take tests to determine their aptitude for certain types of endeavor. Then long periods of education may be necessary to reach certain goals, all of which is for power and glory in this world, storing up "wood, hay, and stubble" that will be destroyed in the fire of judgment because the motive was purely psychological, to bring glory to self.

Are these people happy and contented? Psychiatric practice would prove to the contrary when we observe the neurotic wrecks who are unable to satisfy their unregenerate souls by these driving forces. Their entire lives are anchored in this world. They are not seeking "those things which are above, where Christ sitteth on the right hand of God" (Col. 3:1). All their affections are set on the things of this earth, and they choose to live "after the flesh." The individual whose thoughts are centered on minding the things of the flesh cannot change his thoughts or his ways, because his carnal mind cannot get away from minding the things of the flesh. This is a vicious circle.

Psychologies of Man

Is it any wonder that anxious and fearful patients become frantic when they find themselves ensnared in their own lusts? They have no hope; their souls are in despair. What can they do? What will they do? Like the great masses of the world, they will continue to look to the world, where the evil spirits, governed by "the prince of the power of the air," will continually offer them diversions, hobbies, and amusements, attempting to alleviate fears and anxieties. When this fails, they turn to psychology, psychiatry, and psychoanalysis.

Just because the world is worshiping at the modern shrine of psyche does not prove that God's program is failing to give peace to the hearts and minds of those who put their trust in the Lord Jesus. It simply shows that Satan is battling for the minds of men through his gigantic psychological propaganda, denying that man has a soul and placing therapeutic emphasis on the mind as the seat of fear, anxiety, worry, maladjustment, and nervousness. Only the born-again Christian can understand the diabolic deception in such treatment. It is a bold attempt to wipe out all need for Christianity and force man to believe in his own power. Even the few who express a desire to find God are channeled into a bloodless religion, where psychology of the mind continues to hold sway.

Of course, the world cannot see either the folly or the deception of this line of reasoning, because it does not believe God's Word, which says that "thoughts and intents" (Heb. 4:12), "imagination" (Gen. 6:5), "meditation" (Ps. 19:14), and deceit (Acts 5:4) are conceived in the heart.

Without the presence of the Holy Spirit in man's heart, man formulates a philosophy of life, consistent with the unregenerate heart, which can never give him salvation or peace. When dissatisfied with himself and his philosophy of life, he can only hope to substitute another philosophy, devised by his unregenerate heart, which cannot bring him any nearer to peace than the former. In this state unregenerate patients are helpless to change their thoughts, because Satan controls the meditations of their unregenerated hearts.

Christ Is the Answer

God has given us the remedy for all soul problems. If you have not accepted Jesus Christ as your Saviour, God invites you to accept and believe that the shed blood of His Son was offered on the cross of Calvary to make an atonement for your lost soul. This may seem contrary to what you have believed; nevertheless, we can not be saved by the moral rules made up by ourselves. God has given us the breath of life, and we live on this earth according to His mercy. When He takes away the breath of life, we die and our soul goes to one of two places, according to God's plan. Those who have not believed in Christ's atoning work on Calvary go to hell to suffer everlasting punishment—punishment because God made an offer and they refused it. But those who accept His gracious way of salvation, believing in the shed blood of Christ as an atonement for the soul, are carried to heaven to be with Him for ever and ever.

Some will say, "How can that relieve me of my nervousness? How can that take away my worries about myself?"

After you believe that the shed blood of Christ was made an offering for your soul, God sends the Holy Spirit to dwell in you. He, the Holy Spirit, will teach you to understand the Bible. He will give you a desire to read the Bible. As you study His Word and meditate on it, you will come to see how wonderful He is to make all these provisions for you, so that you are able to fight the evil spirits that come to you to make you doubt God, mistrust Him, and little by little you get to rely on yourself instead of on Him.

Finally you overcome the evil influences of doubt, fear, anxiety, nervousness, and worry by trusting and meditating on God's Word and by walking each day, step by step, in the Spirit, not fulfilling the desires of the flesh. When doubts come —and they will—turn them aside by looking at the cross of Calvary, where Christ overcame Satan and all his hosts who oppress and torment us.

2

NERVOUS CHRISTIANS

Before a certain patient was even comfortably seated in my office, she began to pour forth her anguish in these words:

"I'm afraid I'm having a nervous breakdown. I can't control my thoughts. When I read my Bible, I can't concentrate; and since my prayers go unanswered, I am even doubting my salvation. I have a tight-band feeling around my head which seems to get tighter day by day, giving me the fear that something is going to snap and I will lose control of myself. At times I have thought of doing away with myself, but I know that comes from Satan. Now I am afraid to be by myself. What if I should lose my mind and in a moment take my life?"

Yes, Christians suffer from "nervous" symptoms—anxiety, doubts, cares, worry, troubled thoughts, fears, and bodily tensions. But Jesus said, "Let not your heart be troubled, neither let it be afraid" (John 14:27).

Christian reader, do you understand the meaning of these words, "Let not"? The Bible, from Genesis to Revelation, encourages God's children to trust Him completely and not let cares, troubled thoughts, and anxiety accumulate in their hearts until they are in bondage to nervousness.

Bodily Tension

The Christian who is beset with emotional problems has not come to his state of suffering overnight. This suffering has been a long time in developing—in some cases, many years. The resultant constant anxiety, night and day, over a period of time brings on bodily tensions, which the patient presents to his physician. He is suffering and pleads for relief from one of a combination of annoying symptoms common to so-called nervous patients. These symptoms, even though created by the patient's emotional conflicts, are very real to him and cannot be classed as willful imaginations. The patient cannot shut them out as one turns off a water faucet.

Most patients are aware of the fact that when their fears are intensified, their bodily tensions increase; and when the fears diminish, the bodily tensions gradually subside.

Practically all nervous patients complain of tenseness in the body at some time during their illness; with some it is continual. The area involved may vary—tenseness in the neck muscles, a band-like feeling around the head, or migraine-like pains. Or there may be a tenseness with atypical (not typical) symptoms in the chest or the abdomen, which can be diagnosed only as nervous heart, nervous gall bladder, nervous stomach, or, for want of a more specific diagnosis, dyspepsia, because there is no pathological lesion in these organs that can be successfully treated by medicine or surgery. The indefinite, perplexing symptoms in the female organs, brought on by fears associated with womanhood, have led to much unnecessary surgery for relief of nervousness in women.

Medical practice is constantly confronted with functional conditions which do not have their origin in disease germs, brain disease, or fictitious, run-down nerves, but in the emotional conflicts in the soul, causing fears, anxiety, and bodily tensions.

Don't Blame the Doctor

The so-called nervous patient wants relief from his symptoms, be they mental fears or bodily sensations brought on by fears. Usually the doctor prescribes a nerve medicine. The drug by itself cannot alter the patient's emotional problem; it only dulls the mental thinking so that he is not quite so alert to his fears. As a consequence, the patient feels better, but he is not cured.

Do not blame the doctor for not curing the patient of nervousness, for he did not tell the doctor what made him nervous. Today's nervous, fearful patients are very much like the first patient who complained of fear to his Physician. Adam did not tell God the cause of his nervousness; he related only the symptoms of fear to Him: "I was afraid, because I was naked; and I hid myself" (Gen. 3:10).

The Great Physician did not waste any time with Adam's nervous symptoms—fear, guilty conscience, and anxiety. Neither did He carry out an endless series of laboratory tests. His all-seeing, diagnostic eye was able to look right into the soul of Adam and see the cause of his fearfulness. When God questioned His patient, Adam, He made him face the real fact for the cause of his nervousness, what made him "afraid," by asking him point-blank, "Hast thou eaten of the tree, whereof I commanded thee that thou shouldest not eat?" (Gen. 3:11).

The modern doctor, in spite of his advanced scientific knowledge, is unable to see the cause for the patient's nervousness, yet he knows that there must be a cause for the fears and bodily tensions. As long as the nervous patient hides from the doctor the cause for the functional symptoms, the physician can only assuage the symptoms—fear, anxiety, and tensions—if not of too long standing. Therefore, in most instances nervous suffering is a periodic recurrence of symptoms which may be eased in intensity by various forms of treatment; however, the symptoms are usually reawakened to greater intensity with each succeeding attack when new cares and worries enter conscious thinking.

In Bondage to Nervousness

Worldly Christians, not willing to yield self to the Lord, willfully deceive themselves into believing that the fearful thoughts can be controlled by the will. When this fails (which it always does), they turn to worldly methods and sedatives to divert the thinking processes. The sedatives calm and soothe; the diversions distract the mind; the shock treatments make them forget the symptoms; but none of these therapies deliver them from the source of their suffering, which is the sick soul.

Some patients are outwardly happy when they have been relieved of their bodily tensions associated with fear and anxiety. However, these patients, who from all outward appearances seem to be cured, are in a constant state of apprehension, lest they read about or hear of patients who had symptoms akin to theirs and lost their minds or committed suicide.

Many Christians secretly depend upon sedatives to act as an insulation against their nervous symptoms, instead of yielding self, with its desires, to Christ and walking in the Spirit. Christians should know that no modern drug or physical therapy can change the state of a man's heart or affect the desires of the heart. If the heart is not cleansed daily of its cares and troubled thoughts, these problems accumulate and bring the Christian into a chronic nervousness, which, of course, is not a nerve disease at all, but a conflict in the soul between the old self-will (which should have been crucified) and the Holy Spirit, who came into the soul to make His abode there.

How the Evil One Ensnares the Christian

Nervous Christian patients often ask, "How did this happen to me? I tried to live right."

Yes, they tried to go in their own strength, laboring religiously for God in their strength instead of in His Spirit. Too often Christians are beguiled into believing that they are "laboring in the Lord's work," when in reality the work is being carried out in the strength of self, to the gratification of self, and not to the glory of God. What happened? They did not walk in the Spirit of Christ, reading His Word, communing with Him in prayer, and keeping their minds ever on the atoning work of Christ on Calvary.

When Christians leave out daily fellowship with Christ, they suffer from spiritual malnutrition. If the Christian fails to take the daily requirement of spiritual calories because of worldly attractions and too many religious duties, he soon becomes anemic and run-down, his resistance is lowered, and he is an easy prey for disease (evil powers). Some Christians require more spiritual calories than others, depending upon the type of work, the demoniac hindrances, and how much one desires to please the Lord in a yielded life.

When the Christian succumbs to emotional problems (becomes nervous, so to speak), he has taken his eyes off God and let them drift back to self, until finally, as he neglects the Word, self becomes all-important and God is set aside. The prayer connection is lost. Then the nervous Christian becomes confused, alarmed, and afraid. He tries to pray, but his thoughts remain on self. He tries to read God's Word; but he cannot concentrate, because his thoughts drift to self-introspection. He has no peace of mind, night or day. He even doubts his salvation and is certain that God has forsaken him.

God has not forsaken the nervous Christian, but the nervous Christian has forsaken God. When? When he gradually took his eyes off the importance of Calvary and walked in his own strength.

"I Cannot Read the Bible or Pray"

A Christian woman requested medicine for her nerves, saying, "If I could take something to stop this tightness in my arms and hands, I would not have the urge to pick at my face. It's my nerves that make me do it. I can't stand to have hairs showing on my face. I have been plucking them.

"Little things make me so nervous. If the sweeper gets out of order, I am afraid it cannot be repaired. I am afraid the automatic washer might not work.

"I had trouble like this twenty-five years ago. I was in the hospital with a nervous breakdown. I got over it after so long a time, but this time the doctors cannot find the right kind of medicine. I have been in the hospital, but nothing helps. I had insulin shock; then they gave me electric treatments on my brain. It made me forget things I should remember, but the things I want to forget are stronger than ever.

"Now I don't know what to do. I have thoughts of doing away with myself; but I know I will not do that, because I am a Christian, and the Lord would not let me. Somehow this has gotten such a grip on me that I cannot read the Bible or pray. God seems so far away. I want to be near Him, but my thoughts are never on Him any more. How did I get this way? I seem trapped. But how to get out of it?"

What Made the Patient Nervous?

If this patient had told the Great Physician about all the little things that made her nervous, I am certain that He would have said to her, "Martha, Martha, thou art careful and troubled about many things" (Luke 10:41).

My Christian reader, you need not be a psychiatrist in order to see that this woman was not suffering because of any one particular condition in her life; but she was trapped by many cares and anxieties.

Satan is very subtle in his process of beguiling the Christian with a little worry about this and a little anxiety about that, until the little worries and anxieties have formed an insurmountable mound.

When did the patient's problem begin? She recalls that she had her first nervous collapse (which required hospitalization) twenty-five years ago, but psychotherapy revealed that her trouble began many years before that time.

Over the years she grew careless in her Bible-reading and spiritual meditations, until Satan cut off her spiritual supply, causing her to lament that she could not read her Bible or pray. We blame Satan; but really it is our fault when we let him do it by troubling us with many things. Each trouble, as it arises, must be taken to the Lord and put into His care. Jesus said, "Let not"; therefore, Christians should not let cares and anxieties accumulate in their hearts to worry them and make them tense, or nervous.

Let me repeat that these so-called nervous conditions do not come on overnight. When a Christian lets himself get to the state where he can no longer read the Bible to his soul's gratification, he has wandered away from God. The old self-desires pushed God out of his life.

There is only one way out of this bondage of fear. When the prodigal son came to himself through suffering, he repented, returned, and sought his father's face. Too often I find that the Christians who are unable to re-establish their relationship with God by reading the Bible and praying have not truly repented of their self-will, self-love, self-trust, and self-exaltation. Their only desire is relief from their suffering. They are like my patient who wanted a medicine to take away the uncomfortable feeling in her hands; she was not concerned about the pride that made a compulsion for her hands.

The nervous patient is largely responsible for his condition. He could have done something about it before the nervousness became a fixed habit. He should have confessed his weakness and fleshly conflicts to the Lord.

The Nervous Christian Has No Testimony

The Bible tells us that Christians are the "light of the world," which is manifested by the fruit of the Spirit. "But the fruit of the Spirit is love, joy, peace, longsuffering, gentleness, goodness, faith, meekness, temperance" (Gal. 5:22, 23).

Does the Christian in bondage to self, in bondage to his nervousness, show forth love? No! He is all taken up with self; his self-centered interest will not let him show love for others. He does not even have love for God. He will complain, "No use praying to God; He does not answer my prayer. I can't read the Bible; it holds no interest for me."

Does his life show joy? No! He moans and bewails his oppressed state, from which he claims he wants deliverance.

Does he have peace? No! He runs to and fro in the world, hoping to find a remedy for his nervous symptoms. He portrays a confused, doubtful, fearful mind, being agitated by a soul that is out of fellowship with God.

Does the emotionally unstable Christian demonstrate an attitude of long-suffering? No! He is extremely short in long-suffering. He is short-tempered, short in patience, short in tolerance with others, short in everything that does not gratify self. The man who is all taken up with self is very sensitive. The old self, ego, "I," cannot bear criticism. In the sight of his fellow man he must be approved; he cannot let them think that he is peculiar for Christ's sake.

What about the spirit of gentleness? Can he show gentleness and kindness, help others, and do things for others? No! The sufferings of others seem to annoy him. He will say, "I can't be around them; they make me nervous with their talk." This by interpretation means that their talk interferes with "my thoughts about myself."

Can he show goodness? No! He is like the natural man; his thoughts of self-interest will not let him do things for others. He says to himself, "How will that help me? I will do things for others when I get over this nervousness, but right now I don't want to visit people or talk to them. It is too strenuous. It makes me nervous, because I wonder, while talking to them, what they are thinking of me. I am afraid they will see that there is something wrong with me. It makes me nervous to go to church. I get short of breath and tight all over if the preacher talks loud."

Let us listen to a confession: "I don't know if I am saved. I thought I was, but since I can't read the Bible with feeling and my prayers are not answered, I am afraid that I have committed the unpardonable sin. There is no hope for me; it has gone this way too long." Such patients have no faith in God, and doubt pervades all their thinking.

Does he show meekness? Surely he is not surrendered. He believes that his suffering is a cross which he is bearing for Christ, yet there is no sacrifice or glorification of God in the suffering. How can it be, when he accuses God of unfaithfulness, when he could not be emptied of self? After all, one of the greatest contributing factors to nervousness in the Christian is that self has not been crucified with Christ, leaving a struggle between the Spirit and the flesh because the patient does not walk in the Spirit, but makes provision for the flesh (Rom. 13:14).

And what about temperance? Does he have self-control and restrain himself from "the lust of the flesh, and the lust of the eyes, and the pride of life"? He makes the excuse that he cannot control himself, because he is nervous. But there was a time when he had the choice of controlling his will for Christ or for the flesh. Apparently he let himself be overcome by doubts, anxieties, and cares of this world.

Suppose you were unsaved and had convictions that you needed salvation. Would you turn to a doubtful, fearful, anxious, nervous Christian? I am sure that you would not, because he has nothing that would make you desirous of anything that he has in his life. He could not and would not talk to you about Christ. In the first place, he is not interested in Christ, and he is not concerned about you. His only concern is self.

There Is Hope

Is there any hope for the nervous Christian to overcome his bondage, to be released from the snare of the Devil? Yes! The Lord has undertaken in a marvelous way for those who call upon Him in truth. Many Christians will say, "But my condition is hopeless. I have tried everything." Yet God is able. Will you do your part, as follows?

FIRST: Go back to the cross of Calvary, where you first saw the light.

SECOND: The "I" (self) must be crucified with Christ in order to get rid of the "old man"— self-will, self-trust, and self-sufficiency — which makes you rebel against God's plan for your life. "And they that are Christ's have crucified the flesh with the affections and lusts" (Gal. 5:24).

THIRD: Meditate on what Christ did on Calvary for you. Study the Bible diligently until you grasp the complete picture of Calvary. If you do this, the love of God will dawn upon you.

FOURTH: If you have been nervous and fearful for many years, doubts, guilty feelings, and past sins will return to trouble you by sheer force of habit. Turn to I John 1:9. Study this verse carefully until you get the full impact. Read this verse in relation to its context.

FIFTH: Meditate on God's Word daily, moment by moment, so that you may be able to stand against the wiles of Satan, who will attempt to bring you into bondage again.

The Christian who is a so-called nervous patient, beset with fears, anxieties, worries, and cares, is definitely not walking in the Spirit. The nervous patient who listens to the cries and groanings of his nervous symptoms will be overcome by them, will be bound by them, and will become a slave to them.

Slavish fear drives patients to find some kind of relief. Slaves are not led; they are driven. Satan drives his slaves, but Jesus leads His sheep.

Jesus said, "My sheep hear my voice, and I know them, and they follow me" (John 10:27). What is wrong, then, with nervous Christians? Do they not hear Jesus? Do they not hear Him say, "Why are ye troubled? and why do thoughts arise in your hearts?"

Nervous Christian, turn your eyes from self to Calvary.

3

SO-CALLED
NERVOUS BREAKDOWN

Tschaikowsky, the great composer, suffered much during his lifetime. On one occasion, after a thorough medical examination, he wrote thus to a friend: "The doctors say there is nothing wrong with me; it is just my nerves. But what are nerves?"

The diagnosis, which was puzzling and apparently very unsatisfactory to Tschaikowsky, has bewildered many suffering patients. If there is nothing wrong, and it is just nerves, then why all the suffering, the patients want to know.

Bankers, lawyers, professors, businessmen and women, preachers, housewives, and even nurses and doctors leave the physician's office with this hopeless diagnosis ringing in their ears. The rich and the poor, the educated and the uneducated, men and women from every walk of life, have succumbed to this mysterious malady, the so-called nervous breakdown.

If someone were to ask you what a nervous breakdown is, what would your answer be?

My patients say that a person with a nervous breakdown "goes to pieces," "can't control his

thoughts," "can't control his mind," "becomes un-
glued."

When they come to me for help, their chief
complaints run something like the following:

"I worry all the time. I can't stop it! If it keeps
on, it will wear out my nerves, and they are so bad
already."

"People don't believe me when I say I'm nervous. They don't believe I am ill."

"I am hanging on by a thread."

"On the inside I feel like a watch spring ready
to go 'boom!' "

"If I just had a broken leg, or an operation,
people would see that I am suffering. Now they
think I am imagining I am ill."

"I have such terrible thoughts. I am afraid God
will punish me for such sinful thoughts, but I don't
want them."

"When someone watches over my work, I get
so nervous that I can't control myself. I am afraid I
will cry in public."

"I am afraid I will worry so much that eventually I will not know what I am doing. I am so
forgetful already. If it gets worse, I might commit
a terrible crime and then not be certain that I did it;
and even if I didn't, someone could come and accuse
me, and I would believe I am guilty."

"I am so tense that I have to have an enema
every day."

"I am afraid I am a victim of schizophrenia. I
have all the symptoms. It goes way back to my
childhood, just as the book says."

And every physician hears the cry, "Doctor, I am so nervous!"

These and thousands of other complaints express the perplexity of patients who want to know, "What are nerves?"

They Are Misunderstood

The patient wants sympathetic understanding when he presents himself with this complaint, "The doctors say there is nothing wrong with me. Now my friends and relatives say it is all in my head— just imagination."

Nervous patients are the most misunderstood of all sufferers because of the false ideas that are associated with nervousness. The general attitude of disdain for suffering nervous patients has caused them to hide the fact that they have been diagnosed as nervous. Thousands of patients cling to a minor physical ailment or search for one that can be treated medically or surgically in order to avoid the stigma of being labeled "neurotic." Because there is nothing physically wrong, they are called "neurotic"—as though they loved to be sick, or just imagined an illness to get attention or escape some responsibility. The patient with a neurosis suffers alone because he is not considered ill.

In twenty-five years of psychiatric practice I have not seen one nervous patient who enjoyed his suffering. Nervous patients are like one who said, "I am caught in a trap, and I can't get out of it by myself."

In their desperation to be understood they may secretly, if not openly, express hope for a serious illness or surgery that might lead to death. One patient, suffering from a neurosis most of her life, said, "I was glad to go to the hospital for the operation. Not that I wanted the operation. They assured me that the operation would cure me. I knew it would not, but I had a legitimate excuse to go to the hospital. Furthermore, if I am not going to get well, it would have been a good time to die, as I never could commit suicide on account of my mother and, of course, on account of my brother, who is nervous."

Nervous patients do not deliberately or willfully conjure up symptoms of fear and anxiety. The patient in the throes of fear and anxiety had a basis for the onset of these symptoms, which did not come on suddenly, nor were they created by a crisis in the patient's life; but the symptom complex developed over many years. Sometimes it has its origin in childhood.

The reason we associate a so-called nervous breakdown with a crisis, such as the death of a loved one, financial reverses, loss of position and prestige, etc., is because the added emotional stress is too much for the personality that is already overloaded with emotional complexes. We blame the breakdown on the stress which is most prominent in the patient's life at the time; however, that is only the added "straw that broke the camel's back."

Every individual wants to be considered mentally normal. We are reminded of the modern psychiatric dictum: All nervous patients have much about them that is normal, and normal people have

much about them that is abnormal. Nervous patients
are not mentally weak. Some of our greatest intel-
lects are suffering from nerves.

Dread of Being Diagnosed Nervous

Nervous patients who receive medical or surgical treatment, whether it is indicated or not, have
hopes of relief, even if the medication is only for
the treatment of a slightly subnormal hemoglobin.
In their own thinking they console themselves with
the hope that the doctor found something physically
wrong which is responsible for the so-called nervous
condition. It does not leave them to face their relatives and friends with the supposition that it is
entirely nerves (imagination or lack of mental control)—"all in the head." Thousands upon thousands
of patients rest their hope on daily vitamins to
relieve whatever ails them.

To be told that there is nothing physically
wrong, that it is "just your nerves," leaves the nervous patient to go on the assumption, if he has not
already been told, that he must control his thoughts.
"Don't worry." Sheer will power will fail, which
only helps to increase the fear that his mind, or
thoughts, cannot be controlled and that he will have
the inevitable breakdown.

Before and After Treatment

Nervous patients, because of their personal
fears, are so sensitized to everything that hints of
nervousness that they not only hate their own nervousness but dread being reminded of it by meeting
other nervous people. They even have an intolerance

of each other. One emotionally upset patient said, "I hate nervous people; they disgust me. For that reason I don't want others to see that I am nervous. It makes me tense to appear before people where they can scrutinize my nervousness. I get worse; I get hot all over. I feel they despise me. I watch everybody to see their reaction toward me. I just can't believe that they could like a person like me, because they see my nervousness."

This seems to be the reaction of most nervous patients who are introspective. They dread meeting people, especially other people tied to their emotional problems. They seem to have so little in common with other emotional patients. They all reason that their emotional problem is worse than that of anyone else in the whole world, and that others could not understand how they feel. They even suppose that the psychiatrist never had a case as complicated as theirs. They will ask, "Doctor, did you ever have a case just like mine? Did the patient get over it?"

These very same patients, whom relatives and friends in disgust call selfish, do a complete about-face when they have solved their problems and are loosed from self. They were not selfish during their emotional illness, in the true sense of the worldly selfishness of the unregenerate. They were bound to self.

After their deliverance these patients have another complaint. Please note the change of spirit: "It seems I am like fly paper. I collect all the neurotics from everywhere. They tell me their troubles and expect me to help them. I know they need help.

I know how they feel. I feel so sorry for them, but I don't know exactly what to do for them."

Another former patient said, "It seems that everybody has problems. Almost every person I meet wants to unload. How do they spot me?"

This patient was not peculiar or spotted because of her past neurotic tendencies. Her emotional battle taught her compassion. Her soul understanding inspires confidence in emotional patients to confide in her. Since she overcame, God is able to use her.

If the patient has not sufficiently matured in his Christian growth to trust in the Lord, he will be tempted to go back ever so often to the graveyard of buried problems. He will dig them up and re-evaluate them in the light of his vacillating feelings, rather than in the light of God's Word, which tells us that God remembers our sins no more (Isa. 43:25).

These people also are upset at meeting "problem" people. One patient expressed her reaction in these words: "I wish people with problems would leave me alone. They call on me, and I have to listen to their problems; then I have all those feelings come back to me again, and I don't want to go back to where I once was."

False Conceptions About Nervous Breakdown

The term "nervous breakdown" has a fearful meaning, suggesting breaking down, wearing out, or degeneration of brain cells and nerve tracts of the body. The term is unscientific and very misleading, because emotional, so-called nervous patients do not suffer from nerves that are breaking down, and their minds will not eventually snap.

In fact, the nerves of a so-called nervous person who has suffered emotionally for many years do not show any evidence of disease. This false conception, however, has caused much fear, because anxious patients anticipate brain changes as they become engrossed in their own thinking and lose capacity to control their thoughts.

Immediately this question will arise in the minds of some of my readers: "Can't the mind become diseased, or sick?" The brain is not diseased in patients suffering from emotional symptoms— cares, doubts, anxiety, fears, and worry. When the brain is actually involved in a disease condition causing mental confusion, we name the brain disease which causes the mental condition, such as brain tumor, apoplexy, brain abscess, encephalitis, arteriosclerosis, and syphilis. These organic brain diseases account for only a small part of mental diseases in or out of our mental institutions.

Overwork

Overwork has been blamed as one of the chief factors in the so-called nervous breakdown. This false conception is based on unscientific observation, but traditional beliefs are hard to break. We continue to hear the traditional advice to nervous patients, "Don't work too hard, now. Take it easy."

Insisting that the restless, agitated, nervous patient lie down and take a rest every afternoon can be actual torment for him. He is forced to commune with his fears and control the bodily tension which could be wisely released by his working.

When nervous patients believe that their work is too hard for them, they demand shorter working hours. They are mentally exhausted because they try to carry on their regular work and at the same time devote part of their thinking to their anxieties. Eventually the work is too hard, because their emotional conflicts require so much of their thinking time that they cannot devote any time to their labor.

A certain foreman in a plant became morose and spent much time by himself. Gradually he became less efficient in his work. The company, on the assumption that he was working too hard and was headed for a nervous breakdown, insisted that he take a six-week vacation. Little did the company realize that their employee, a married man with a family, was unable to carry out the plant orders because he was mentally occupied with the problem of carrying on illicit love relations with another woman and was being haunted by the fear that his wife would detect his dual life. When his moral convictions finally made him break off relationship with the second woman, his working habits improved.

Shorter hours and less days of labor a week should lessen the number of nervous-breakdown cases if overwork is a factor. Emotional upheavals, however, are on the increase, as though idle time and attempting to satisfy the desires during idle time create more problems. Man has no standard by which to establish rules regarding overwork. God, however, gave Adam to understand that he was to work and earn his bread by the sweat of his brow. But nowhere does He tell him not to over-work, lest he have a nervous breakdown.

Study Too Hard

Every psychiatrist in state mental institutions has heard this explanation from relatives as the reason for the mental illness of a newly admitted patient suffering from schizophrenia:

"The patient had his nervous breakdown be-cause he studied too hard. He made good grades until some time before his breakdown, a year or a year and a half ago. Then we noticed that he studied harder, but he began to fail in his work. Then he became antisocial and wanted to be by himself. He quit school because he was failing in his studies. He began to act peculiar. He sat around laughing and talking to himself when he felt that no one was watching. Finally he became uncooperative, resistive, and refused help of any kind."

Thus when he is admitted as a schizophrenic patient, he is controlled by hallucinations and delu-sions which did not come on overnight. In his heart he fantasied and imagined thoughts which at first he could brush aside when it was necessary to concentrate on his schoolwork. But eventually the fantasies became stronger, because the indi-vidual desired the pleasurable sensations derived from thoughts, until it gradually became impossible to set them aside for the daily duties of life. Nor did he desire to set them aside, because they were more pleasurable than the tasks of life, which lost their importance to him.

The schizophrenic patient has lost interest in the things in this world because he has created for himself a world of fantasy in which he has everything as he has imagined it in his heart. In his lucid moments and by fragments of conversation his mouth reveals the abundance of fantasy that completely controls his heart.

The psychiatrist, by detailed history-making, is convinced that the hallucinations and delusions were a long time in the making and that there was no brain disease that was the exciting factor for the mental illness. Yet the parents will endeavor to blame the mental illness on various incidents in the early life of the patient, such as falling out of a crib, falling down the stairs, a bad fright, or a severe illness.

Periodically scientific research comes up with a new theory that suggests that there is a germ or a chemical in the brain which is responsible for the bizarre mental symptoms. To date, from the psychiatric viewpoint, the suffering from schizophrenia, manic depressive psychosis, and emotional problems of adjustment is influenced by the individual's environment and not by any alteration of brain structure.

From the Christian viewpoint, when the mental confusion is not due to an organic brain condition, the symptoms are basically expressions of what the heart has generated. When the heart is cleansed and an individual walks in the Spirit, the patient has a normal, right mind. It is self that loses stability and goes out of control. The Spirit does not go out of control.

Insane Over Too Much Religion

Satan definitely has a hand in creating this illusion. He does not condemn religion, but he teaches that you can get too much religion and "go overboard." However, all his followers have a religion. Religion is man's philosophy of life. Every uncivilized heathen has his religion, which is compatible with his thinking and way of life, and Satan drives him to fanaticism. Likewise, he drives the cultured heathen to be loyal to his religion, serving evil spirits that oppose the atoning work of Christ on Calvary.

Satan does this by teaching that the way of the cross of Calvary is foolish, absurd, queer, and unreasonable to normal intellect. To the unregenerate, who do not have the spiritual discernment, this diabolic teaching seems reasonable. Not only does Satan point out that such teaching is absurd, but that those who believe such a gospel are queer. No one wants to appear or be considered queer. Therefore, Satan gets people to frown on those who walk according to the teachings of the Son of God, as if they were immature for needing someone to lean on, instead of standing on their own rights and privileges.

The subtlety lies in the fact that Satan makes the teaching seem so reasonable and applicable to the unsaved and to nominal Christians: "But if our gospel be hid, it is hid to them that are lost: In whom the god of this world hath blinded the minds of them which believe not, lest the light of the glorious gospel of Christ, who is the image of God, should shine unto them" (II Cor. 4:3,4).

Satanic influence blocks the attempts of the Holy Spirit to draw unsaved ones to God by showing them how unliked by the world they would be if they became Christians. They have no incentive, therefore, to investigate Christianity for fear of losing their standing among men.

It is not uncommon to find mentally disturbed (insane) patients talking incoherently about religion. Many of these patients spent considerable time in religious talk and ritual before their final state of mental confusion and incoherence. Therefore, it is only natural for unsaved people to conclude that they went insane over devoting too much time to religion.

Before these patients became incoherent, they were probably misguided into bloodless creeds, which did not satisfy their souls, but confused them; and they are trying to find peace through their religious rituals.

Admonishing patients who supposedly went insane over too much religion not to talk religion and taking the Bible from them is not the remedy for their confusion. They have not had an overdose of the Word of God. They need guidance in understanding what the Bible says about the Way to peace for their troubled souls.

No man ever went insane over Christ, or too much reading of God's Word, or because of communion with Him. God earnestly desires that we think and meditate on His Word, and He promises to answer prayer on the ground that "ye abide in me, and my words abide in you" (John 15:7).

The Biblical saints of old did not go insane because they meditated on the laws of God. God gave this direct command to Joshua: "This book of the law shall not depart out of thy mouth; but thou shalt meditate therein day and night" (Josh. 1:8).

David, a man "after God's own heart," meditated on the law day and night. Moses, God's leader of His people, the Israelites, communed with God "in the mount forty days and nights." Daniel, "greatly beloved" of God, mourned and prayed for his people for twenty-one days. There is no record of these men suffering from nerves because of their continuous fellowship with the Lord.

God's Word does not say that if you have your mind all wrapped up in spiritual things, you will become confused and go insane over too much spiritual meditation; but "he shall be like a tree planted by the rivers of water, that bringeth forth his fruit in his season" (Ps. 1:3).

What is the fruit? Fear and confusion? No! It is love, joy, and peace (Gal. 5:22).

Shed Blood of Christ Scares Children?

Christian children's workers are being faced with the accusation that if they teach little chil-

dren about Christ's death on Calvary for the salvation of souls, the children will be scared and
emotionally traumatized. This teaching, religion-
ists advocate, will make the children nervous and
will be the basis for nervous breakdown later in
life.

Everyone dreads the idea of mental breakdown; therefore, the evil forces hold forth this false
idea that teaching the shed blood of Jesus will
make children nervous. They do not object to
children's workers' teaching that Jesus was a moral
man who went about doing good, but they object
to the teaching that He is our Saviour, "because
of Calvary." The trick is boldly evident! Take
away the shed blood of Christ on Calvary and we
have no salvation.

This is just another of Satan's lies, propagated
by his own, who hate to hear about the blood shed
for sinners. It is the adults, not the children, who
are afraid of the blood.

I have never heard any adult patient blame his
fear or nervousness on teachings of the shed blood
of Christ on Calvary. I have had patients tell me,
however, that when they were children they worried for years, fearing that the world would come
to an end and they would go to hell. Other patients
have told of childhood fears of dying, being buried
alive, going to the bad place, and the fear that God
would not have them in heaven because their parents would not forgive them.

Satanic forces in various disguises are always
active to hinder the spread of the gospel, whether

it is given out to adults or to children. Satan will do anything and use any means to hinder the teaching of the shed blood of Christ on Calvary for the remission of sins.

Adjusting

Many Christians who suffer from so-called nervous breakdown have a fear of psychiatric treatment because the academic psychiatrist applies the same treatment to Christians as non-Christians— adjustment to the world.

The Christian's problem is spiritual, and Christian patients cannot make an adjustment to the world and be at peace, for they are no longer of the world after the Holy Spirit has come to make His abode within them. Jesus said of His disciples, "They are not of the world."

Christians who desire to make an adjustment to the world turn with their problems to counselors who will confirm their way of life, so that they will not feel guilty for turning from Christ to the psychologies of man. The worldly Christian may experience some relief by means of sedatives, diversions, and other forms of man-devised treatment; but as long as the agitating factor, feeling of guilt, remains, it continues to build up emotional tension until the body suffers. (This suffering will be discussed in another phase of this writing.)

The spiritual Christian, however, has a relationship to Christ, and he yearns for the re-establishment of fellowship with God. When psychotherapy brings him to an understanding of his

problem, it is not difficult for him to see that his
deliverance is in confessing his sins to God, who
"is faithful and just to forgive us our sins," and
in casting all his anxieties, worries, and fears upon
the Lord Jesus Christ.

The natural man, who yearns for fellowship
with the world, can make an adjustment to the
world because he is "of the world." He can again
become occupied with the things that satisfy and
give pleasure to self. But they give him peace only
"as the world giveth." He has no convictions that
he needs to confess to God, and although his confessions to man cannot cure him of the condition
that makes the pressure, he experiences relief when
he releases tension by confessing guilt feelings
which he has repressed for a lifetime.

One patient expressed her relief in these words:
"Now I have told someone! I never thought I would,
or could. You don't know how much relief that has
given me. I kept those things to myself all my life.
I could not tell a soul."

Confessing for the sake of releasing pressure
is comforting at the time, but this can become a
habit. Many patients use the psychiatrist as a
"spillway" when there is too much pressure
dammed up.

Christian patients, however, have a repugnance
toward hashing and rehashing unpleasant, sinful
incidents of childhood—perhaps showing up their
parents' sins and weakness. This rehashing even-

tually builds up hatred and resentment for the parents, and possibly an unforgiving spirit.

One Christian patient said, "I would like to learn how to be forgiving, rather than to overstress the weakness and mistakes of my parents. That only builds up resentment toward my parents. After all, considering their personal emotional problems, they did the best they could."

A long-drawn-out course of analyzing subconscious layers of thought is not necessary for the Christian. I realize that many of my Christian readers who have delved into psychology, hoping to find a solution to their problem, will wonder what finally becomes of the complexes of childhood that are somewhere down in the "sub . . . sub." Let me explain that these complexes, which, according to academic teachings, are in the subconscious, are, according to the Word of God, in the heart of man.

When Christ enters into the individual's soul and self is crucified, the symptom complex common to nervous patients will not develop in typical textbook style, because the Christian then goes in the power of Christ instead of self.

The Christian cannot get by with transposing his cares, worries and anxieties, and guilt and fear from the heart to the unconscious mind, or to a mysterious subconscious, so that he can resort to mind treatments of forgetting and covering up.

These thoughts and feelings are more than mind deep. SO-CALLED NERVOUS BREAKDOWN IS A MISNOMER FOR EMOTIONAL CHAOS IN THE SOUL OF MAN.

4

PSYCHOSOMATIC SUFFERING

When the "nervous" patient is under a continuous strain of fear and anxiety for a long period of time, the tension may release itself through and into various parts of the body, causing physical symptoms and disease conditions, and sometimes death. In other words, so-called nervous conditions do not always remain in the mind as worry, but may produce physical symptoms and organic diseases—somatic diseases.

Therefore, when the emotional (psyche) state causes bodily (somatic) disturbances, we call such a condition "psychosomatic."

Psychosomatic symptoms signify that the individual is having a war within himself. This warfare has created emotional tensions which can affect any part of the body (soma).

Nervous tensions may be the whole cause, or at times only the exciting factor, of certain forms of eczema, sweating hands and feet, warts and skin rashes, allergies, asthma, hypertension, nervous heart, dyspepsia, nervous stomach, gastric ulcer, chronic gall bladder, chronic appendicitis, vomiting spells, hiccoughs, diarrhea, constipation, mucous colitis, spastic colitis, rectal conditions, urinary disturbances, certain forms of arthritis, goiter, migraine headache, painful and irregular menstrual cycles, and sexual problems in both men and women. Yes, worry can involve the whole body.

Pride and Psychosomatic Illness

Even though the term "psychosomatic" pertains to the body as well as to the emotions, it nevertheless suggests and carries with it all the old stigma associated with the term "neurotic." Unfortunately, this gives the impression that one having a psychosomatic condition suffers from a personality inadequacy as well as a personality conflict. Since no one wants to be considered weak, either in his own eyes or in the eyes of his friends, he is reluctant to be regarded as psychosomatically ill. Having to say, or to have it said, that he has an organic illness caused by his nerves implies that he is not able to control his thoughts, or that he has a weak will.

Patients with a psychosomatic condition are just as reticent to seek help for their emotional problem as the so-called nervous patient, who is controlled by fear and anxiety.

Showing or giving way to emotions is considered a weakness. This is cultured into our makeup as children: "Don't act like a baby! . . . Grow up and act like a man! . . . Stop your crying! . . . You are a baby."

Adults laugh without restraint, because laughing was never taboo; but they are afraid to show grief or to mourn for loved ones. A certain minister goes about among his members admonishing those

who show a tendency to mourn, "Don't give in to
your emotions; don't let yourself break down." The
person who is sensitive to the words "break down"
takes it to heart. saying to himself, "I must not
break down. I might go out of control" (have a
nervous breakdown).

Patients have no difficulty in going to a
physician when they want relief from suffering
brought on by organic symptoms. But going to a
psychiatrist is a different story. Patients usually
have their guard up. They want relief, but they are
afraid that the psychiatrist will find something
about them that is not very nice. After all, we all
have a degree of respectability about our lives and
want to be liked.

A certain married woman had periods of un-
predictable blind spells which were not only annoying but dangerous, as they might come on
while she was crossing a street in traffic. She
had a long history of nervousness before the blind
spells came. Special eye study proved that she had
no organic condition to treat. This left her with
the diagnosis that the blindness was entirely nervous.

Psychiatric study gradually revealed that these
symptoms first appeared when her husband came
home late in the evening. She did not have eye
trouble when her husband did not go out for the
evening.

She was a Sunday school teacher and was
terribly embarrassed to have her Christian friends
know that at times her husband came home in-

toxicated. She hoped that it was not so; therefore, when he came home late, she refused to see his condition by having a convenient blindness, so that she would not be able to look at him. At first this was convenient in helping her to protect her pride. But the habit grew until suggestive thoughts would provoke the blind spells at any time, night or day, when her husband was not around.

Just explaining the cause of her blindness to this patient did not automatically cure her of her problem. Psychotherapy had to bring the patient to an understanding of the fact that pride (what would people think?) was the basic factor in her suffering. The patient had to be willing to realize that just creating blindness to a situation had not convinced her mind that her husband did not become inebriated.

For peace of mind and soul it is best for us to admit that no one is perfect; and when faced with our imperfections and trying circumstances, we should admit that they are true.

Hostility and Physical Suffering

Emotional tensions caused by hostile motivations hidden in the heart are sometimes expressed in burning sensations in the skin. A young lady, employed in an office of a large plant, suffered from a number of open skin lesions on her body. She admitted that she produced the lesions by scratching because of unbearable burning sensations. Before she came for psychotherapy many remedies had been applied, locally and internally, to allay the itching; however, the treatments had not brought any lasting relief. It was observed that the itching lesions occurred only on parts of her body which were readily accessible for scratching while she was at work.

During psychotherapy the patient soon told about an unwholesome situation at her place of employment. Another girl, whose character was questionable, was sharing the office work in the parts department; but she did not carry her share of the burden and spent much time loitering around with the manager (male) of the department. This left the patient to do more than her share of the work.

The patient readily recognized the fact that the burning of her skin and her need for relief by scratching were tied in with her hatred of the other office girl, who was favored because of her immorality. However, being a Christian, the patient was a little reluctant to see that her skin condition was a repressed rage, burning inside her because she did not dare voice her feelings. Nevertheless, she was surprised that her itching and burning lessened in intensity as she learned to accept her position without hatred and realized that "vengeance" for immorality "belongeth to the Lord."

It is not unusual for psychosomatic patients to go through many medical and physical examinations before they are convinced that they are psychosomatic and need psychiatric help.

A married woman, also with a skin condition, made the rounds of physicians for relief of itching skin. It seemed that any remedy, when first applied, gave her relief and sustained her for some time, as new remedies always seem to give hope to patients for a while.

The patient said, "I tried to bring up all the symptoms I could to the doctors to keep them interested; for as soon as they found out or decided that I was nervous, they lost interest in my case. Then they turned me over to the nurse for routine shots of either a sex hormone or calcium. When they gave me the allergy tests and agreed that there was nothing unusual, that I was just slightly allergic to a few things, I saw that I was out of luck again."

This patient was a Christian; but while discussing her problems in a general way, interjecting her Christian views, she gave no evidence or clue to the problem until she expressed her regrets toward her husband's lack of consideration for her in their conjugal relationship. Then it became visibly evident why she scratched her arms, face, and neck. During the consultations she scratched her arms until they bled. She sheepishly admitted that she wanted to scratch her husband for his "demanding without love" attitude, but she knew that she did not dare scratch him.

This is another case of suppressed rage in which the patient directed the hostility against herself, lest she direct it to the object of her hatred and suffer retaliation. She said, "If I should strike him, he would strike back; he is stronger than I."

The patient was relieved of her need to scratch herself when she and her husband realized that their basic difficulty was lack of consideration for each other in all matters of married life.

It Is the "I"

The dermatologist sees many patients suffering with various forms of dermatitis, eczema, and other forms of rash, which are difficult to relieve by local treatment, because the emotional tension from within the psyche keeps the skin irritated. The driving urge to accomplish more than is humanly possible is often manifested by the sweating of hands and feet. Is this drive exerted to glorify God? No. It does not come from the Spirit. It is the old ego, "I," trying to accomplish something to please self. The Spirit does not cause psychosomatic suffering. Remember, it is the "I" that causes all the trouble. It is the "I" that gets irritated, filled with hate, rage, and envy, until it expresses itself as a psychosomatic disease. The "I," not the Spirit, makes us sick.

Psychosomatic Pain and Surgery

Psychosomatic conditions are not new. They have always been in existence, but it is only very recently that medicine has recognized the fact that the emotions can make us suffer physical pain and cause disease conditions which destroy the body (physical death).

Thirty years ago our medical schools taught that stomach ulcer was caused by some irritant in the stomach. They frequently cited the following illustration to substantiate their theory: In China stomach ulcer was observed in men, but seldom in women. The men in that country ate at the first table, thus eating hot food; while the women ate after the men had been served, having to eat cold food. The hot food was supposed to be the exciting factor in causing stomach ulcer in the men.

Today medicine generally accepts the psychosomatic idea that some individuals under specific types of distress develop stomach ulcer. Something is worrying them, or as we often say, "eating on them." The worry eats on the stomach, or on the duodenum, as the case may be.

A young man who was a plant manager grew up in very straitened financial circumstances. He had a strong drive to get away from his boyhood poverty; therefore, he was ambitious to make a place for himself in the world. He advanced rapidly in the industry in which he was employed, but with continual fear that he would eventually be set aside because other men had a college education, whereas he had only completed high school.

The inevitable happened. A man was called in from the outside to fill a position which, according to seniority, should have gone to the patient. His nervous stomach, which had been giving him gastric distress intermittently, developed into a gastric ulcer.

The patient was treated from a surgical viewpoint. His vagi (nerves going directly from brain to stomach) were cut, thus intercepting the impulses of hate, rage, sense of injustice, and fear, generated in his heart, which came up to his mind. Culture and expediency had not permitted him to express his heart thoughts, but as the irritation continued to build up, it had to be expressed somehow and somewhere. The repressed impulses ate on his stomach, because he dared not pour them out on whom it might concern.

The operation, from all outward appearances, gave evidence of success, because the emotions could no longer send impulses to his stomach to bite, to churn, to rage. Was he cured of stomach-ulcer symptoms? Yes, but the rage was still fomenting in his heart, sending impulses to his mind.

Several years after the operation this patient sought psychiatric help for a fear that had been growing within him for some time. As he put it, "I am afraid people will notice that there is something wrong with me, and that I might show my nervousness to the company bosses. They would lose confidence in my ability because I am mental.

"When I look at myself to see how nervous I am, I get feelings. When I am afraid my legs won't carry me, my legs get numb, and I know I walk awkwardly. When that passes off, I wonder if my hands are all right. What if they would shake when I take notes at the directors' meeting?

"I am in a mess! If these conditions get so bad that I can't go to work, I will lose my job. Then I won't have the money to support my family. I will have to sell my house and move into a cheaper neighborhood. What would happen to my family's social standing?"

After he spent several months out of the state and six weeks in a hospital, with various types of accompanying therapy, the source of this man's fears was not changed. He was ready to turn to Christianity after he had tried practically everything the world had to offer to divert his mind. All the therapies and diversions failed to give peace to his turbulent and insecure heart.

When he turned to his early Christian training, he gradually forsook the conventional religious reading "stuff" which seems to gravitate to these tormented souls. It seems that these people, once led astray by mind-appealing religious literature, need to be tutored in Bible-reading in order to get rid of the psychological interpretations that they want to place on God's Word.

When this patient came to trust in Christ's finished work on Calvary, he gradually learned to depend upon God to supply his daily needs. "But my God shall supply all your need according to his riches in glory by Christ Jesus" (Phil. 4:19).

Neglecting the Psychic Factor

If medical and surgical treatment of psychosomatic diseases does not consider the psychic factors involved, the patient may be relieved; but he is not cured, as was so evident in the preceding case. The aggravating cause continues to pour poison (anxiety and tension) into the body. Eventually the patient suffers again, the last state being worse than the first.

The ulcer patient, whose suffering we have discussed, was relieved of his ulcer symptoms by surgery, but his ambitious desires for himself (his sin) were not checked. He continued in self and eventually came up with a worse condition—physical symptoms and mental illness.

The Great Physician warned one of His psychosomatic patients that a worse thing could happen to him if he continued in sin. We read in the fifth chapter of John that when Jesus healed the impotent man of his bodily infirmity at the pool of Bethesda, the man did what his Physician told him to do—he took up his bed and walked. Later Jesus met his patient in the temple and warned him that if he continued to be controlled by the sin that had made him suffer for thirty-eight years, he would be afflicted again; and he would be worse off than before. "Afterward Jesus findeth him in the temple, and said unto him, Behold, thou art made whole: sin no more, lest a worse thing come unto thee" (John 5:14).

If you will acquaint yourself with the work of the Great Physician as He healed the souls and bodies of the suffering ones, you will find that He treated other cases of psychosomatic suffering. Yes, psychosomatic suffering is an old disease.

Psychosomatic suffering is a vast field of medicine. Therefore, it has not been my purpose to write a treatise on psychosomatic medicine, but to show the reader that when nervous Christians do not daily cast their cares upon God, but try to go in their own strength and let worries accumulate, they suffer in the body.

5

THIS THING CALLED FEAR

Practically all patients who come to the psychiatrist present one outstanding basic symptom—fear. The following fears, expressed by souls that are out of fellowship with God, are samples of fears revealed by my patients:

"I do not know if I am saved. Years ago I thought I was; now I don't know. I don't know the exact time it happened. How do I know if I believe in my heart?"

"Sickness scares me; it brings me so close to death."

"I am afraid to die. It is such a lonesome feeling, leaving everybody, going out and wandering about in the unknown."

"I have committed the unpardonable sin. I know I have, for God does not hear or answer my prayers. I want to kill myself; I am lost anyway."

"I have a tight, band-like feeling around my head, and the muscles in my neck are so tight, I am afraid something is going to snap in my head if I don't get relief soon. I am keyed up all the time. I get frightened. I am wondering how long my mind can take it."

"I am afraid to take Holy Communion, afraid I will take it unworthily."

"I am afraid I will pass out or black out, and people will see that there is something wrong with me."

"I have a constant fear in my heart. I felt I was going to black out. I came very close to it several times, but I never fainted. I got so nervous, my eyes twitched; then I was afraid to read, afraid my nerves would break down and nerve exhaustion would cause blindness."

"I am afraid I will go berserk and kill someone."

"I am afraid my mind will snap at some inopportune time and place and I will commit a crime."

"When I am in a mixed group, I am afraid I will be driven by an uncontrollable urge to be indiscreet around men."

"I am afraid of losing my mind because of these uncontrollable, dirty thoughts."

"I can't forgive myself for telling my mother that I was away at school while I was having my baby out of wedlock. My mother died before I came back. I feel I must destroy myself."

"I am afraid my baby will be marked because of what I did to myself."

"They say I am like my father in so many ways. I am afraid that if I marry I will have an unsettled married life like Father had. I am afraid to fall in love."

"I am afraid I might go insane over religion. I saw two students crack up in Bible school. What's to keep me from losing my mind?"

"What would happen to me if my mind would snap while I am day-dreaming about assaulting little girls?"

"I am afraid people are noticing that I am not right, especially since my father said to me, 'Where is your mind? You walk around in a blank.' "

"I know I should quit taking sleeping pills; but I am afraid doctors will take them away from me, and I won't be able to stand it. I am afraid I am a drug addict."

"I am afraid people will find out that I am coming to you. They will watch me to see if they can find out what is wrong with me."

"I am afraid I will lose my job; then I would have to sell my house and move into a cheaper neighborhood. I would lose my social standing."

"I am afraid to go to sleep. I am afraid I might die in my sleep."

"My heart pounds, and I have trouble getting my breath. But, oh, how to stop it!"

Of enumerating fears there is no end. In twenty-five years of psychiatric practice I have heard these cries of fear, and many variations of them. *Every person who seeks the counsel of a psychiatrist is driven by fear.*

What Is Behind These Fears?

When a physician is confronted with a sick patient, he always asks himself, "What made the patient sick, and where is the disease condition?" He also questions the patient as to how long he has been ill and asks him to describe his symptoms. Likewise, the psychiatrist, when confronted with a patient expressing a fear, asks himself, "What is back of this fear? What started this fear?"

Usually the sufferer will answer his counselor as Adam answered God, by giving him the fears and symptoms as they affect him at that moment. In many instances the fear is hidden behind the physical symptoms which it has caused, making fear the responsible cause for many organic diseases.

It is necessary for the counselor to urge the patient to give a history of his suffering in order that they can see together how the sufferer has been rationalizing and doping his mind with drugs to cover up his worries.

Probing Into the Emotions

Psychotherapy is not a pleasant ordeal. The physician who does the probing must be very careful lest he probe too deeply and strike a sensitive nerve, so to speak. If he does, the sufferer will flinch by saying, "Oh, no, Doctor! I don't think that is the condition in my case. It is not my fault. Others are to blame."

Does this sound strange to you? Perhaps you think that you would not be guilty of such an excuse; but Adam was, and so are all his descendants.

While the Christian counselor is weighing the facts that the individual is giving forth, it is essential that he evaluate the stage of that person's spiritual development. At what point in the patient's spiritual growth did the devouring dragon stand in his path before him and whisper doubts, which caused him to take his eyes off God and become concerned about himself? The more introspective and doubtful he becomes, the less he depends upon the "armour of God," until he becomes bound to self, finally overcome by the adversary.

When the evil forces cause the Christian to break his fellowship with God, the Christian suffers, manifesting symptoms of fear and anxiety—so-called nervous symptoms. If this spiritual state is not corrected immediately, it will not be long before bodily tension and physical symptoms also make their appearance. This latter condition is, of course, harder to overcome than the former, because the patient overemphasizes the bodily symptoms as the cause of his nervousness, forgetting what caused the bodily symptoms in the first place.

By way of illustration: Adam told his Physician that he was afraid because he was naked. Adam was making a big issue of his bodily symptom, nakedness. He insisted that the nakedness made him afraid (nervous). God turned him back to the time when he took his eyes off Him, when he meditated on Satan's lie (doubted) and was overcome by Satan, when he ate of the forbidden tree. Likewise, in Christian counseling psychotherapy cannot be successful unless we know when, where, and how the adversary withstood the Christian in his spiritual development.

The patient might be relieved of his symptoms by the use of tranquilizing drugs and much reassurance, giving him to believe that he is cured. But unless the patient knows when and how the adversary catches him off guard, he has no protection and continues to live in a state of fear.

Reactions of Christians

Christians who seek psychiatric counseling separate themselves into two groups: those who seek information about their problem; those who seek confirmation of their way of life.

When the spiritual Christian comes for psychotherapy, he is willing to go right to the point. He does not resent the counselor's efforts to bring him face to face with the facts. He is willing to examine and evaluate his attitude toward God with a sense of humility and eagerness to please God. He sincerely desires to seek God's face and fellowship with Him. The spiritual Christian is cooperative and makes a speedy recovery.

When worldly Christians come for treatment, they cannot readily be distinguished from the nominal Christians, the professing Christians, the professing church members, or from those who belong to the "mixed multitude," who associate with God's people and imitate the visible part of religion without faith.

Worldly Christians definitely desire approval. They are not humble, and they insult God by setting up a standard for themselves. Of this the Apostle Paul writes when he says that those who commend themselves measure themselves by themselves and compare themselves among themselves. They usually resist God and have a sense of rebellion, as though the evil spirits that beguiled and overcame them are driving them against everything that comes from God; and yet they feel that God should be more benevolent toward them. Especially is this true of those who have been out of fellowship for a long time.

These people resent probing into their problem and show hostility on the least pretense, projecting all failures in the treatment onto the counselor. This reaction is an old satanic influence which was first revealed in Adam.

When God told Adam the cause of his fear, did Adam accept it? Adam immediately tried to change the subject and blame someone else. In fact, he was very impudent. He not only blamed his wife, but he told God that it was really His fault for giving him such an unstable helpmeet: "And the man said, The woman whom thou gavest . . . she gave me of the tree" (Gen. 3:12).

Too often sermons on this subject make a joke at the expense of the woman, thereby hiding the real lesson that we are to read in this verse; namely, that Adam blamed God for his sin. This hateful, rebellious attitude expressed by Adam after he was out of fellowship with God has its parallel in the Christian of today who is out of fellowship with God and is being energized by Satan to go in his self-will. While in this state Christians may be impudent, unlovable, and uncooperative toward those who attempt to help them, because they are being energized by evil influences sent by the "prince of the power of the air" to control them.

First Sin—First Fear

It is clearly stated that the Lord God came to the garden to talk with Adam in the morning, "in the cool of the day." But after fear overcame Adam, he avoided God by hiding among the trees. Of course, we know what made him afraid. He had eaten of the forbidden tree, having rebelled against God. Rebellion against God is sin.

Do we read that Adam was afraid before he partook of the forbidden tree? Was he afraid before he sinned? This is the key that my Christian readers must use with which to evaluate the problems of guilt, worry, anxiety, so-called nervousness, or nervous breakdown, and many other problems associated with the mental suffering of those who are overcome with fear.

The man or woman who fears is not in complete harmony with God, for "perfect love casteth out fear" (I John 4:18).

Emotional Pattern for All Generations

When Adam turned from God, he set up an emotional pattern to take care of guilt, fear, and sin which is being used by his descendants even in this present generation, six thousand years later.

Adam did not turn to God, whom he had offended, and ask for forgiveness; but he proceeded to cover up his guilt and sin by turning to his own devices. In Genesis 3:7 we read: "They sewed fig leaves together, and made themselves aprons." This was Adam's solution to cover their nakedness and their sin.

Self-devised schemes to cover sin have no lasting effect on the guilty conscience. Sedatives and the new tranquilizing drugs dull the brain; lustful pleasures divert the mind from cares and worries, and hobbies keep the mind occupied; but all are temporary measures devised by man.

Fearful (nervous) patients seem to get some release while they are doing something for themselves. This urge to be doing something is a satanic drive to keep the mind occupied. But self-devised schemes for covering sin cannot give peace to the mind as long as the soul has not been cleansed of guilt. *Nothing less than the shed blood of Christ on Calvary can cleanse the guilty conscience.*

We have no record that Adam feared while he loved God and communed with Him. He feared after he sinned. Spiritual Christians testify to this scriptural truth today: As long as they love God and meditate on His will for their lives, they have no fear. "There is no fear in love; but perfect love casteth out fear" (I John 4:18).

When the spiritual Christian fears, he searches his heart to see what iniquity is standing between himself and God. The worldly Christian, on the other hand, because he loves the world more than God, will devise a scheme "which seemeth right unto a man" when he desires to please the old lustful nature.

When nervous (fearful, anxious, worried) individuals are tempted to turn from God, they are not blind. They are as conscious of breaking their fellowship with God as Adam was when he sinned. But like Adam, they go from one homemade covering to another. Because God is long-suffering and does not consume them when they turn their affections from Him to Satan's world, they believe that they are successful in their own devices.

By keeping themselves occupied with their devices, they are able to sear their conscience for many months and years until they are past feeling, or until it dawns upon them that they are overcome with fear of fears. Then they cry out for help, making their friends believe that their nervousness (fear) came on suddenly. *It never comes on overnight.* They have been going from one device to another until there are no more devices to quiet the struggling soul that has been so long away from God. Then patients cry out, "God is so far away; I can't reach Him. He does not hear my prayers."

Fear—Lack of Faith

Basically all Christians with fear have a common denominator—they are out of fellowship with God. With the first suggestions of fear, they should realize that they are not walking close to God. They do not have on the "whole armour of

God" and are not carrying "the shield of faith" with which to "quench all the fiery darts" of Satan —the darts that create doubt and fear.

When Christians neglect to take unto themselves the "armour of God' for their protection, they take their eyes off Jesus and turn to self; then they become bound to self (become slaves of Satan), withered branches which no longer draw sap from the vine and no longer bear fruit.

A Christian overcome by fear has lost his testimony for God. This is not God's fault. Many sufferers, unable to make contact with God in prayer because they are out of fellowship, accuse Him of punishing them in this manner. Without doubt this is a subconscious feeling of guilt. Yet Christians are reluctant to accept the suffering as their own fault. Remember, it was not God's fault that fear came upon Adam; *he brought the fear upon himself.*

It seems that most Christians, after suffering for many years, just assume that God has overlooked and forgotten the time when they turned to the world and forsook their "first love." Most of these patients have really not repented of their backsliding, but have taken on religious works as a covering for sins.

The Word of God specifies that the most important part of the "armour" is "the shield of faith": "Above all, taking the shield of faith, wherewith ye shall be able to quench all the fiery darts of the wicked" (Eph. 6:16).

Overcome With Fear—Bound to Self

A person who is overcome with fear, obsessed with fear, tormented and agitated constantly by fear, does not have a free mind. He cannot open his mind to listen to what is said to him. His mind has been overcome with fear of fears. He imagines that just a little added fear will carry his mind into a state of mental confusion in which he is separated from his friends. Then he might commit crimes and acts beyond his control, which would only further alienate him from those about him. As one fearful patient expressed it, "I am afraid I would become a wandering star that is doomed to 'blackness of darkness forever,' floating around in space until I struck something."

When a person reaches such a state, he is indeed a problem to deal with. His whole being has been turned from light to darkness—from Christ to self. Everything he hears, sees, feels, or thinks suggests a fear that will overpower him. When he reads the newspaper, his eyes seem to have an uncanny alertness to pick out all words that hint of mental conditions. Words such as "insane," "suicide," "berserk," "neurotic," "mental," and "asylum" seem to appear in boldface. He is compelled to read the news item against his will; he must know what happened to the individual and how closely the case fits his condition. Should the information have dire forebodings, the reader is worse off for having read it.

However cautious he may be to avoid contacts and suggestions that might incite fear, he is certain to encounter them at every turn of the way, for he cannot live in a vacuum; furthermore, he would be afraid to be isolated, afraid of fear thoughts that might come to him.

During a conversation he picks out doubtful phrases which he applies to himself. A friend, while making plans for him, might say, "When you get well, you can do thus and so." He grabs at the word "when," which to him suggests uncertainty, perhaps doubt, as to whether he will ever get well.

However, if he consults a psychiatrist who comes up with new therapy, there is always hope. especially if the psychiatrist can place some eminence to the therapy by saying that it is used at a famous medical center. But if the treatment has previously been a failure in his case, he is afraid that the psychiatrist has run out of luck and is just experimenting.

To those patients overcome with fear and bound to self, prayer and Bible study will have little or no appeal. They believe that their well-meaning friends are turning to religion as a last resort. Their attitude and their capability of grasping the spiritual depend upon their past spiritual condition, whether religious, stony-ground believers, or spiritual Christians who took their eyes off Jesus when Satan had worldly circumstances beguile them to attempt to go in their own strength. Whatever the case may be, the person out of fellowship has turned to reason; therefore, he will hope for a magic escape from fear.

The fearful person is so completely absorbed with his fears that his mind is able to grasp only a small portion of what is spoken to him. This means that the greater portion of his thinking is bound up with self.

Bound to Self—Bound to Satan

I am writing expressly to spiritual Christians at this point. I am aware of the fact that the church is almost silent on the subject of "demons and evil powers." Yet the Bible, from Genesis to Revelation, is plain in the teaching that Satan, "the prince of the power of the air," and his host of evil emissaries oppress God's children.

Men and women possessed with fear of fears not only demonstrate that a powerful influence has them bound to self, but they frequently express it in words. As one patient expressed it, "I am caught in a trap. But how to get out of it? I can look back and know how I got there, but it was so gradual, over the years, that I did not realize my plight until I was caught. I want to get well. I want help from you, but something tells me to scream, 'No! No!' when you talk about Jesus."

Another patient said, "My head goes around in a whirl. I am afraid my mind will go blank if I listen to you."

Not only do the evil forces, activated by the "prince of the power of the air," influence, oppress, torment, and bind God's children who are careless in not wearing His "whole armour," but when Satan binds them to self, he uses varied methods of keeping them in his control.

When they attempt to return to God, he discourages them by blocking their prayers and hindering the reading of the Word.

A familiar misconception, which is generally accepted as a scientific fact among non-Christians, is that if the patient struggles to read the Bible and prays to God, he may go insane over religion. This falsehood has turned many honest seekers from the Lord and has kept many Christians spiritually emaciated because they were afraid to search the Scriptures for the truth. *No one ever went insane from reading the Bible or because of fellowship with God.*

To Whom Shall We Go?

One day Simon Peter asked Jesus a question which every Christian would do well to ask the Lord when it becomes necessary for him to find help in time of suffering: "To whom shall we go?"

Spiritual Christians do not expect non-Christians to help them with their problems of fear and anxiety, because they know that non-Christians cannot understand soul problems. They usually want to be very sure that the counselor is a born-again Christian who loves the Lord, and it is not unusual for them to ask him if he is a Christian. One Christian who tried to make certain about this matter before she began treatment put the question to me in this way: "What is your relationship to the Lord?"

Christian counselors are "ambassadors for Christ," interceding "in Christ's stead" for those

who are overcome with fear. It is God's redemptive
love in Christians that makes them able to intercede
with Him for other Christians who are in bondage
of fear, always bearing in mind that it is only
through God's grace that we ourselves have been
taught and strengthened to appropriate the faith
of God, thereby being able to avoid the pitfalls
which caused them to stumble into traps.

Realizing that often we are blind to the subtle
snares that cause us to stumble, let us not sit
as a judge over such Christians, but let us be
compassionate. "Remember them that are in bonds,
as bound with them" (Heb. 13:3).

With this attitude toward those who are anxious and fearful, the Christian counselor inspires
confidence in them to see his desire to help them.
This is the first and greatest hurdle that the sufferer must overcome before he can trustingly reveal
what he has so carefully concealed from everyone.

The worldly Christian, who has broken his
fellowship with God and become fearful, having lost
confidence in himself and also in his fellow man,
tries to find someone whom he can trust, someone
who may not necessarily be a Christian. During
the process of psychotherapy he learns to trust his
counselor. Rapport is essential if the treatment is
to be helpful to the patient.

The counselor imparts what is in his soul,
influencing the soul of the patient to Christ, or to
a deity away from Christ. There is no neutral
position! One is either for or against Christ.

Many carnal, worldly Christians believe that
they can be cured of their so-called nervousness by

modern psychological therapies. Patients may be helped by these treatments and relieved of some symptoms, but this does not deliver them from fear and guilt. I have never seen them lifted out of their worldly state or drawn any closer to God by the psychological reasoning of man. Diverting the fear, covering up the fear, or forgetting the fear cannot bring peace to a soul and relieve his guilty conscience. Only by overcoming the fear through the shed blood of Christ can the conscience be cleansed of guilt, freed of fear, and the soul find peace.

Psychiatric patients are reluctant to seek help before they are overcome with fears. They seem to be determined to keep all their thoughts, actions, and reactions under cover and are willing to endure for years before they can muster up enough courage to select the counselor who they believe will agree with their philosophy of life.

The more worldly the Christian is in his Christian walk, the more he resents hearing the truth that caused his fear; and he is very cautious in his selection of a counselor. Worldly Christians are prone to turn to the psychologies of man, which give peace to the sufferer "as the world giveth"— an adjustment to this present world and away from Christ.

Some patients are controlled by more pride than others; the ego, "I," self-esteem, must be guarded. How often have we heard this remark, "I would not want to go to my pastor; he knows all about me!" Instead the sufferer goes to someone who does not know him, so that he can tell the counselor only what he wants to tell him in order to frame the plan of thinking of the counselor. This deceit in the heart of the sufferer accounts for many failures in treatment and is the reason why many continue to be in bondage to fear for a lifetime.

It is not unusual for sensitive Christians to decide quite suddenly, even during the period of psychotherapy, "Now I believe I can go home and work out my problem by myself. I know what I must do." But they do not. Sooner or later they go elsewhere for treatment.

Patients who have been "let down" in prior consultations tread warily at first, to be sure of their ground. Patients sometimes say, "I told him everything, and then he did nothing for me." . . . "He took me apart but could not put me together again."

These situations are unfortunate, but the Christian should not expect non-Christians to help him with his problem. It is unfair to expect them to understand spiritual things, which can be discerned only by the Spirit of God within the Christian. It is rebellion on the part of God's redeemed children, who are blood-bought, to turn from Him to the world with spiritual problems.

Christian, remember that when the Lord asked the disciples if they also would go away (to the world), Peter himself answered the question he had asked by saying, "Thou hast the words of eternal life" (John 6:68).

The spiritual Christian trusts Christ to lead him as our earthly fathers took our hand and led us over difficult and dangerous obstacles. That did not take away the object of fear, or make us forget; but we were no longer afraid, because we trusted our fathers. And so, since we are in Christ, He leads us to overcome.

Confession

The person who relates a symptom to his counselor is not confessing. Did Adam confess that he ate of the forbidden tree and was guilty of death? No! He gave God a "symptom," which came on as a result of his sin: "I was afraid, because I was naked; and I hid myself" (Gen. 3:10). Likewise, all sufferers invariably first confess to the counselor the symptoms, which are consequences of what is hidden. "Fear hath torment" (I John 4:18), and they want relief from the torment (fear) which is punishing them.

The fearful patient wants his conscience cleansed from anxiety and guilt. This cannot be accomplished by treating symptoms. The patient must confess the sin which makes him guilty. But confession must be based upon something more substantial than a psychological release, which many people experience by merely confessing something. If there is to be a lasting therapeutic value in confession, the patient must come to the understanding that only confession from the heart and repentance toward God will bring healing to his soul and peace to his mind.

Confession does not imply a lengthy analysis of the subconscious memory. Neither should there be a lengthy rehashing of all the evil, lustful imaginations, making sin a commonplace thing rather than something to be loathed. The matter of delving into the subconscious layers of rationalization is necessary and valuable for the patient only insofar as it helps him to understand how he got himself so hopelessly bound to self. But a long-drawn-out course of analyzing the various subconscious layers is not necessary for the Christian.

The Christian is not trying to divert each problem into new channels, but to see how he was led to stray from God and to find his way back to Calvary. The patient should acquire an understanding of his way of life—how Satan was able to ensnare and devour him, and how to avoid a recurrence of his symptoms. When Jesus healed the impotent man at the pool, He later sought him out to remind him to be careful how he walked henceforth: "Sin no more, lest a worse thing come unto thee" (John 5:14).

Prayer

Prayer and fellowship with God through His Word are essential for the Christian if he is to overcome his fear.

The spiritual Christian who has permitted his worries and anxieties to interfere with his prayer life knows that he is fearful because he has not been casting all his care upon the Lord, and that he has permitted the cares of this life to come between him and the Lord. But he needs the help of psychotherapy in order to understand how, when, and where Satan beguiled and ensnared him, so that he may know just exactly what to pray for.

He soon realizes that it does no good to cry out to the Lord for relief of his suffering until he has been healed of the cause of his suffering. He has come willingly for psychotherapy, is very cooperative, and soon grasps the fact that his suffering is more than mind deep, that it reaches down into his soul, and that there is nothing wrong with his mind.

With this understanding of his problem, the spiritual Christian soon finds that his fellowship with the Lord through prayer and reading of the Word has overcome his fear.

The worldly Christian presents an entirely different problem in psychotherapy. To him prayer is more or less a psychological or emotional exercise which should miraculously relieve him of his fears. He vaguely hopes, but does not really believe, that prayer can accomplish anything for him.

He would much prefer a "religious" counselor or treatment by academic psychiatry; but because of pressure brought on by relatives, he resentfully comes, with the hope that the Christian counselor will, after all, approve of his way of life.

He does not see that his suffering has anything to do with his spiritual state; therefore, if there is to be any praying, he expects the counselor to do the praying. But unless, or until, he changes his attitude, prayer is of no avail in his case, because

God has a definite prerequisite for answered prayer:
"If ye abide in me, and my words abide in you, ye
shall ask what ye will, and it shall be done unto
you" (John 15:7).

The carnal Christian presents a real problem
in psychotherapy. He is obsessed with fear, bound
to self, and completely wrapped up in himself. His
own words tell us that he has lost connection with
the "Power House," and that he feels lost without
that help. Does he not often say, "I cannot read my
Bible or pray"? And he cannot.

He cannot pray, because the nervous, carnal
Christian's thoughts concern only one person—
himself. Prayer involves two persons—the individual who prays and the One to Whom he prays.

The carnal Christian expects some sort of
therapy to cure him very quickly, and his prayer
is, "Lord, take away my suffering." Psychotherapy's big problem with the carnal Christian
is to help him see that his suffering was a long time
in developing and that he cannot expect a few
psychiatric consultations to do anything miraculous for him.

The carnal Christian needs to go back . . . back;
for it is usually a long way back to the place where
he lost his "first love." The Lover of his soul has
been pushed into the background, and he has become his own lover.

Be compassionate with the carnal Christian
who is overcome with fear. Do not excuse yourself
for not interceding for him by saying, "Pray about
it. You must have faith." He has heard this over

and over again. If it were so easy, he would pray
and get his suffering over with. He cannot pray
himself out of his trouble, because he does not
know what to pray for.

Confession, Repentance, Salvation

The following case history, drawn from my
earlier experience in private psychiatric practice,
is cited here, not only to portray a certain patient's
foreboding anxiety concerning things to come in
the hereafter, but also to show how God's hand
was at work trying to awaken me to understand
fear as soul anguish rather than a mental process
which might be eradicated by academic psychiatry.

The patient, a young married woman living
with her husband, mother of one child, and several
months pregnant at the time, was afraid that her
unborn child might be marked or born deformed.
After considerable questioning and discussion, she
revealed a fear that such an affliction might come
upon her new baby because she had formerly committed an abortion.

At the same time she pleaded for relief from
a tormenting fear that overwhelmed her night and
day—a fear of death and going to hell. Usually
the fears were worse at night, overpowering her
in the early morning hours after sedatives had
worn off. During the day she could brush her fears
aside by keeping her thoughts diverted to the
affairs of the day.

Several nights during the time of psychotherapy, before the fear could be overcome, she

was awakened by terrifying dreams and could not go back to sleep. She frequently called me at two or three o'clock in the morning to relate her fearful reaction to horrifying dreams in which she was on the verge of being cast into hell.

The dreams all evolved around the central idea of being punished in hell for her wicked way of life. She related several dreams; but one dream in particular repeated itself, with only slight variations, several times during the early part of the illness.

THE DREAM: The patient was riding a bicycle in a grooved rim that circumscribed a large globe representing our planet. A person sat on the globe, acting as "master of ceremonies," directing her activities, which he did with a sense of sadistic glee, because he had her in his complete control. On the outside of the rim, away from the planet, was utter blackness; churning smoke, flames of fire, and offensive odors were rising from the black abyss. She could hear babies crying, people moaning and pleading for mercy and relief from the torment of hell. There was a nerve-racking sound of utter pandemonium coming from the deep-sounding cavern.

The master of ceremonies forced her to ride around the rim at a great speed, demanding that she make a specific number of rounds before the gong sounded, or else she would be cast into hell. While riding, she had to answer riddles. Failure to give the correct answer caused her to lose her balance, and she fell over the rim into space. Then she would awaken with a panic and could not go back to sleep for fear of a repetition of the dream.

She was obsessed, night and day, by the idea that she could smell burning hair and scorching toenails, which she described as the offensive odor like that which comes from placing a hot horseshoe on the hoof of a horse while fitting it before nailing it on the hoof. She heard people crying, moaning, and pleading to be released from torture—from somewhere below the earth. (End of dream.)

When the patient's olfactory senses were activated by fear, she believed that she saw smoke rising. During consultations she sipped water every few minutes to relieve her hot, dry, burning tongue. When she seemed intensely fearful of hell, there was little, if any, evidence of saliva.

Some of the patient's symptoms suggest the story in the sixteenth chapter of Luke. One might surmise that she had heard this story and was convicted of her sins. But she insisted that she had never heard it before I read it to her from the Bible, after she had related her dreams associated with hell. She had never been to church or Sunday school, as far as she could recall.

Now let us look into her background. Her entire life was tied to underworld activities. Her father, brothers, and husband belonged to an organization of bootleggers. She was a contact for an abortionist in another town. The life of the family was influenced by a fortuneteller who had an uncanny ability to reveal underworld activities and predicted the death of a brother of the patient

—which happened. The fortuneteller told the mother of the patient that the patient was visiting a psychiatrist.

At the time this patient presented herself, because of my training I was desirous of keeping myself well within the field of academic psychiatry. However, I realized that this patient was presenting a problem which was not of the mind, but of the soul. To be sure, the mind was expressing bizarre statements; not that the mind was sick, but because the soul was sick and suffering, the mind expressed the inner conflict.

Academic psychiatry accepts the above symptoms as the fabrications of a "sick" mind. But sedatives, reasonings, exhortations, and diversions gave her only temporary peace—"as the world giveth." In spite of my training in academic psychiatry, I yielded to my inner convictions by sending her to a revival meeting which was in progress at the time. One evening when an altar call was given during the meetings, she went forward and received Christ as her personal Saviour.

One of the dreams which she related shortly after her salvation expressed the hope and confidence of heaven rather than fear of death and hell. She dreamed that a dangerous flood was surrounding her home, which in the dream was located on a low island. Her husband borrowed a motor boat with which to take his family to safety. Even though there were whirlpools and dangerous waterfalls to navigate, she was certain that she and her husband and one child would reach shore safely.

She did not want to let her husband return the
boat, lest he might not return to his family. (He
was not saved at this time.) Later in the dream
she found herself, her husband, and their four children walking peacefully along the beach of a beau-
tiful country. (In real life she had one child and
the unborn baby.)

When the patient was asked to give her ideas
associated with the four children, she explained
that in the dream she was carrying a baby in her
arms, and it was a perfect baby. (Before her salvation she had a fear that her baby would be marked.)
Then she suggested the possible ages of the two
dream children as somewhere between her oldest
child and the baby. After some thought she said
that the children who would have been born if she
had not resorted to abortion would be the ages of
the children on the beach in the dream of the new
country. Then she confessed that she had two
abortions, instead of only one, and that she had
almost lost her life with the second abortion, which
made her decide to go through with her present
pregnancy.

In her first dream she saw herself wearing a
gingham dress while riding the bicycle. It was the
dress she wore when she had the second abortion
performed, which almost proved fatal. Her associated ideas in regard to the master of ceremonies
in the first dream revealed that he reminded her
of the abortionist, whom she detested vehemently
because he not only demanded a fee for his serv-
ices but also robbed her of her jewelry and took

privileges with her before he performed the abortion. She was furious, but helpless, as she could not retaliate because of her illegal implications with him.

This patient made a remarkably rapid recovery after she grasped the full meaning of the atonement of Christ's shed blood on Calvary for her sins. She became a new creature in Christ Jesus, breaking away from her former life. She no longer had any fear of being punished for past sins, no more fear of hell, no more dreams of hell. *Her mind found peace, because her soul was at rest in the Lord.*

Overcoming Fear

The fears that people talk about have their roots in the fear of spiritual death—separation from God. The Christian who permits the cares and anxieties of life to come between him and God until he is in "bondage again to fear" is afraid because he feels separated from God.

Then what shall the Christian do when he is afraid?

The Christian who is afraid must turn his thoughts back to Calvary and get a vision of Christ's redemptive love for him. He must meditate, moment by moment, on what Christ did and how He overcame. Remember that the fear was built up over a long period of time; therefore, do not expect the thinking pattern to be changed suddenly. The deliverance and being kept from fear is a moment-by-moment dependence on Christ's faithfulness.

But not all fear is bad. There is the fear, a God-given instinct, through which He protects us from potential dangers to our bodies. Were it not for this, we would frequently be injured. This does not imply that we should live in daily fear of what may happen to us, but it does mean that we need to trust God for our physical safety. Nothing can happen to the Christian that Christ is not concerned about, for He lives in the Christian.

Do not think it strange, Christian, that you sometimes fear. Many of the Biblical saints were troubled with fear, but they were not carried away with or overcome with fear. The Apostle Paul says, "Within were fears" (II Cor. 7:5); but he did not let them overtake him. He overcame the fears by the Spirit of Christ, which indwelt him.

"Fear" and "fear not" are not paradoxical to the believer. There is a fear spoken of in the Bible which can be experienced only by the spiritual Christian. "The fear of the Lord" is not a dread, as the phrase might imply. It is not a dread of God's wrath. It is, rather, a deep, reverential awe and an all-enveloping desire to serve Him, to be with Him, and never to be separated from Him.

THE FEAR OF THE LORD DISPLACES ALL OTHER FEARS.

6

MIND UNDER THE BLOOD

Multitudes upon multitudes of people, including Christians, are beset with worry, cares, anxiety, doubt, and fear. And yet when these suffering patients present their symptoms to the physician, he finds nothing physically wrong with the brain and the nerves of the body. Even after months and years of more or less continual worry and anxiety, the brain of the one in bondage to fear is not worn out, nor does it show any pathology (diseased tissue). And so the physician, at a loss for terminology that will explain the patient's suffering, says, "You are just nervous."

But what is "nervous"? And where, then, is the basis for all this so-called mental suffering?

Thoughts Arising in the Heart

Modern man thinks of the mind as the seat from which emanate all men's thoughts. But God's first reference to the thoughts of man points out the fact that the thoughts are imagined, invented, or conceived in the heart: "Every imagination of the thoughts of his (man's) heart" (Gen. 6:5).

The Great Physician, when He foresaw the fear and anxiety of the circle of men about Him on the eve of the betrayal, did not warn them against permitting their minds to be disturbed over the events which should soon come to pass. He said to them, "Let not your heart be troubled, neither let it be afraid."

However, three days later the hearts of these men were filled with fear—fear of man, fear of an uncertain future—and they were gathered together with their friends behind locked doors "for fear of the Jews." When Jesus suddenly appeared in their presence, "stood in the midst," they were "terrified and affrighted." He calmed them by saying, "Why are ye troubled? and why do thoughts arise in your hearts?"

Should not Jesus know where the thoughts of men arise? Does He not know from whence come the anxiety, worry, and fear of man? "All things were made by him; and without him was not any thing made that was made" (John 1:3).

Jesus repeatedly refers to the meditations and imaginations in the hearts of men. On one occasion when He healed the sick, "there were certain of the scribes sitting there, and reasoning in their hearts." Jesus does not say anything about their mental attitude toward Him. He tells them very plainly that the evil thoughts which they had against Him were imagined in their hearts. "Why reason ye these things in your hearts?" (Mark 2:8).

God is always concerned about the heart of man, for "out of it (heart) are the issues of life" (Prov. 4:23). Jeremiah tells us that man receives his just recompense for good or evil deeds according to what comes out of his heart: "I the Lord

search the heart . . . even to give every man according to his ways, and according to the fruit of his
doings" (Jer. 17:10).

God has always known the "thoughts and intents of the heart." He does not waste His time
analyzing the many subconscious layers of repressed thoughts, fears, and guilts, for He knows
what is in man's heart. He told the first man,
Adam, what was hidden in his bosom (Job 31:33).
Adam was afraid after he rebelled and ate of the
forbidden tree; then he complained to God that he
was afraid because he was naked. God did not
suggest any treatment for the mental symptoms
of Adam. He knew that the sudden consciousness
of his nakedness was merely a symptom, or evidence, of what was in his heart. Therefore, He
provided the remedy—blood—for the sin which was
in the heart of Adam.

As the mind of Adam responded to that which
was in his heart, so the minds of his progeny have
reacted to the condition of their hearts. Man has
always attempted to cover up what is in his heart.
Modern man tries to cultivate his mind and intel-
lectually guard his words so as to carefully conceal
what is in his heart. For example, we often hear
something like this: "I was careful not to let my
attitude be known; no one knew how I felt about it."

But modern man may unknowingly reveal what
is in his heart. Have you ever released your tension
by telling someone what you thought of him and
then related the incident, saying, "I gave him a
piece of my mind"? You did not give him a piece

of your mind; you merely exposed the nasty feeling in your heart.

Bitterness and hatred, sorrow and grief, worry and care, anxiety and fear, may be concealed in the heart until it overflows with the burden, and "out of the abundance of the heart the mouth speaketh."

Spiritual Christians do not stumble over the fact that "out of the abundance of the heart the mouth speaketh." They understand that the Lord Jesus Christ refers to the spiritual heart of man— "the inner man." The prophets and the Biblical saints of old understood this clearly and were very conscious of the importance of their heart thoughts, because God "knoweth the secrets of the heart" (Ps. 44:21). The Psalmist did not ask the Lord to search his mind for stored-away evil, but he said, "Search me, O God, and know my heart: try me, and know my thoughts" (Ps. 139:23).

Again the Psalmist cried, "Create in me a clean heart, O God; and renew a right spirit within me" (Ps. 51:10). He knew that the thoughts which came to his mind out of the depths of his heart would be clean if his heart were cleansed.

In the Book of Daniel we read that King Nebuchadnezzar asked Daniel to reveal to him the content of a dream. Daniel, under the divine inspiration of God, not only interpreted the dream but explained the origin of the thoughts which prompted the dream. He said, "O king, thy thoughts came into thy mind upon thy bed" (Dan. 2:29). Now if the thoughts came into his mind, they must have come from somewhere. Where did they come from? The answer is found in Daniel 2:30: "And that thou mightest know the thoughts of thy heart."

It is the carnal Christians who are confused about the heart and the mind. They have acquired their worldly viewpoint by associating with the unregenerate, who avoid the heart and soul of man, thus making the mind the master of man's destiny. "Man looketh on the outward appearance," and so far as the worldly man is concerned, the acts and deeds of man are the products of his mind; "but the Lord looketh on the heart" (I Sam. 16:7).

The Christian who has lost his "first love" and who loves the things of this world more than he loves the Saviour whose blood redeemed him is double-minded. He can speak and act piously when associating with a religious group; but a few hours later, or even a few moments later, he says and does the things that please the unregenerate, for "out of the same mouth proceedeth blessing and cursing" (Jas. 3:10).

But the Word of God says that "these things ought not so to be" among Christians. God cannot use a double-minded Christian, because his testimony does not ring true; and so He says, "Purify your hearts, ye double minded" (Jas. 4:8). Even the world cannot depend upon the double-minded Christian, because he is "unstable in all his ways."

Sooner or later the double-minded Christian is in conflict within himself, because "the flesh lusteth against the Spirit, and the Spirit against the flesh" (Gal. 5:17). His guilty conscience besets him with worry, anxiety, and fear. What does he do then? He goes to a psychiatrist. But from a scriptural standpoint, it would be unprofitable to treat the mind. Why treat the mind for mischief of the heart? This, of course, the carnal Christian does not want to see, and the natural man cannot understand.

The spiritual Christian is anxious to know the truth about his anxieties and worries. As soon as psychotherapy helps him to understand why he is anxious and worried, he realizes that he has not been casting all his care upon the One who can deliver him from all his fears. It does not take many consultations for him to acquire an understanding of the fact that the warfare is spiritual, and therefore of the heart, and that his mind is not diseased.

Satan's Darts

"And they that are Christ's have crucified the flesh with the affections and lusts" (Gal. 5:24); but too many Christians seem to forget that self must be crucified daily, moment by moment, if we expect to "walk in the light, as he is in the light" (I John 1:7). This is the conflict within ourselves; but there is also a conflict from without, being waged by satanic forces striving to enter the mind of the Christian.

We have heard it said that we cannot keep the birds from flying around our heads, but we can prevent them from building nests in our hair. Likewise, we cannot prevent the evil spirits from coming to our minds and whispering doubts; but we can prevent them from getting into our thinking process, not by fighting the evil spirits in our own power, but by submitting to God. The armour of God, the whole armour, is our defense in this battle against Satan: "Wherefore take unto you the whole armour of God, that ye may be able to withstand in the evil day, and having done all, to stand" (Eph. 6:13).

"Stand therefore"; that is, be always ready, lest the adversary catch you unaware and in a weak moment of discouragement cause you to doubt. Thoughts such as the following may come into your mind suddenly without provocation: "Maybe I am not saved. . . . How do I know I am saved? . . . Do I have the proper feeling? . . I do not feel like I did when I was first saved." (Then you try to work up a feeling.)

These thoughts have come to some: "I am afraid that I will want to willfully sin against Christ. . . . I am afraid that I will associate vulgar thoughts with Christ."

Another very common torment which can only come from the Devil is, "How do I know that I have not committed the unpardonable sin?" There are many others, but the above are some of the most common doubts that come to my patients.

What brings these patients to a psychiatrist? They fear that the continual anxiety and worry over such thoughts (salvation doubts) will cause a "nervous breakdown." They seldom realize the origin of these sudden, mysterious thoughts; but Christians naturally are worried about such accusations from the accuser. When their doubts continue and dominate all their thinking, they fear that there is something wrong with the mind, forgetting that "God hath not given us the spirit of fear; but of power, and of love, and of a sound mind" (II Tim. 1:7).

A Sudden, Mysterious Thought

A certain Christian woman, while walking down a city street, saw a dog and was suddenly confronted with the foolish thought, "There goes Jesus. Call to Him. Call, 'Jesus!'" Then she thought, "What if I could not get that disgusting thought out of my mind and God would punish me for being so sacrilegious!" Suddenly the dog stopped and looked in her direction, which only added to her eerie feeling. She had no rest from this thought, day or night. She fought the thought in her own power, which is what the evil spirit desired of her.

Her physician found nothing physically wrong to account for her nervousness. Medicine relieved her tension for a while, but it did not change her thoughts. The patient was encouraged to go to a psychiatrist, who, not being spiritually able to discern her soul problems, gave her the following instructions: "You are overly religious. You had better avoid religion in all forms until you get over this. If you can't control it, we may have to give you some electric shock treatments."

When told that she must give up her religion (Christianity is just "religion" to the worldly-minded), she became agitated and depressed. She wanted to comply with the psychiatrist's request in order to get well, but at the same time she could not turn her back on God. In this dilemma she turned to a spiritual pastor, who advised Christian psychiatric counseling.

All Christians have had similar unholy experiences. These thoughts come to the mind from the atmospheric air, populated by evil-spirit forces. They do not arise out of your heart and come to your mind. By the suddenness of its entrance into your mind, you should be convinced that you did not wish or premeditate the undesirable thought.

As is typical of most spiritual Christians, there was no need for hours and hours of psychotherapy, digging after so-called "layers of unconscious fears." She soon saw her need to go back to Calvary and meditate on her relationship with Christ and what He did for her—not only saving her, but overcoming Satan by His precious blood. Then she appreciated and applied James 4:7 in its proper sequence, as given to the Christian: "Submit yourselves therefore to God. Resist the devil, and he will flee from you."

When we read God's Word, communing with Him about what Jesus did for us at Calvary, considering His love, atonement, grace, and cleansing power, we are resisting evil spirits. Remember that Jesus resisted the Devil by quoting Scripture.

Too many Christians do just exactly what Satan anticipates: They resist satanic influences by their own effort and will power instead of submitting to God and relying on His power. The individual who has been redeemed by the blood of the Lamb and whose whole being—mind, body, and soul—is under the blood has within him the power of the Holy Spirit to resist the Devil.

Anxious, nervous Christian patients ask, "Can the evil spirits return?" Yes! They may, but we have the finished work on Calvary as our hope and comfort for all times and occasions. The Christian life is a continual battle. But be of good comfort, nervous Christian, and remember the words of the Lord God to Joshua when He commanded him to pass through Jordan and possess the land: "Be strong and of a good courage; be not afraid, neither be thou dismayed: for the Lord thy God is with thee whithersoever thou goest."

Something Inside Made Me Do It

The natural man is not equipped with the power to resist the evil spirits or to control the evil imaginations of his heart.

A young married man, the father of a child, was a successful interior decorator by trade. One day a five-year-old girl came into the new house where he was working. He started a conversation with the little girl and soon found himself entertaining and fondling her. He was overcome by an impulse to assault her sexually. In his eagerness to carry out the impulse, yet repulsed by a negative impulse when the little girl tried to release herself from his unnatural fondling, he let her slip out of his grasp, and she ran home to her parents.

When this man was picked up by the police, he was mortified and embarrassed because he was

caught for immorality. He kept repeating, "I don't
know why I did it. Something inside me made me
do it." The law-enforcement body considered it
strange for a supposedly normal man to resort to
such a bizarre sex act and agreed that he should
see a psychiatrist. He played up the idea to everyone who might be concerned that this was a sudden,
impulsive act. In fact, his friends were so surprised
at his perverted conduct that they would not believe that he could commit such a crime and be in
his normal mind. They excused him by saying, "He
must have blacked out. A normal man would not
stoop to such an act."

Let us bear in mind that this man made a normal adjustment to the world in which he moved.
He held a responsible position, worked every day
before the assault, was working when arrested,
continued to work while undergoing psychotherapy,
and has worked ever since. He went to church, as
he said, "as much as the average of my group. I
don't go overboard over religion, but my wife and
my little girl go regularly."

When he was questioned as to whether he
had ever entertained any idea of assaulting little
girls, he talked freely about how, while doing his
routine work, he fantasied about assaulting little
girls and how to seduce women. He reveled in the
sexual excitation that went with such meditation.
He admitted that he had formed a habit of thinking
sexually and evaluating women from their sexual
desirability. He was quite positive in his attitude
that he had a perfect right to think on what gave

him pleasure. He cited how others gave freedom to their pleasurable thoughts: "The drinker drinks to release his thoughts; a man dances with the woman who gives him pleasure; a man picks a movie that lets him satisfy his mood." These were all rational reasonings for an unregenerated man.

Neurologically and organically there was nothing wrong with the brain and the nerves of this man. His mind did not snap. He did not go berserk. He did not have a nervous breakdown or become temporarily insane. His mind did not black out when he assaulted the little girl. He knew what he was doing in every movement of his criminal act.

He willfully permitted his mind to meditate and fantasy on the evil imaginations which were conceived in his heart, and out of his heart proceeded evil thoughts, fornication, adultery, lasciviousness—assaulting little girls (Matt. 15:19; Mark 7:21). Out of the abundance of his heart he finally let his mind be overpowered. Did not he himself say to the police and to me, "Something inside me made me do it"? Little did he realize that he was actually telling us a scriptural truth—that it was his heart's desire that made him do it.

The world and the psychologically-minded pondered about his mental faculties; however, Christians understand that this man's crime was not due to a sick mind, but that his deed was the overflow of evil thoughts from his heart. The evil imaginations had to have an outlet, and he had made provision for the gratification of his lust ("provision for the flesh, to fulfill the lusts thereof") by meditating upon his fantasies until he was continually watching for the opportunity to bring them into actuality.

The Bible says that "the imagination of man's heart is evil from his youth" (Gen. 8:21); out of the abundance of the evil heart comes the constant urge to express evil thoughts and deeds. *An unsaved person has no assurance that the evil imaginations of his heart will not someday overpower his mind.*

Satan Battling for the Minds of Christians

Even when we claim deliverance by way of Calvary, "the prince of the power of the air" continues to battle for the control of the mind from without. To make this clear, let us turn to the Apostle Paul's concern for the mind state of the Corinthian Christians. He says, "I fear, lest by any means . . . your minds should be corrupted." Then he explains how this can come about: "As the serpent beguiled Eve through his subtility," and "if he that cometh preacheth another Jesus . . . or if ye receive another spirit . . . or another gospel" (II Cor. 11:3,4).

Evil forces speak today as they did in the days of Paul. They use apostate preachers to speak to the minds of the listeners, creating all manner of doubt in their minds. If the faith of the Christians is not well-rooted, the doubt can create anxiety, fear, and worry. If the Christian, however, is well established in the gospel of the grace of Christ, he will not meditate on the doubts; therefore, they cannot become rooted.

Christians do not seem to realize that this spiritual conflict is going on daily, sometimes hourly—yes, even moment by moment. One spiritual Christian was harassed almost constantly with the thought of doubting every Christian who tried to help him. He said to me, "How strange! I seem to want to doubt what my wife says, what my pastor says, and what you say. The same holds true for the brethren of the church who want to help me; but I don't doubt my boss or those I work with at the plant."

For two days it was impossible for this patient to read the Bible with any degree of satisfaction, but he could read religious and church literature without much distress. This oppression (oppression and depression are not the same) lasted in varying degrees for several weeks; but he suffered acutely for two days, although he carried on his secular duties.

When Christians are worried, they are not aware of this spiritual warfare and too often turn to mental-hygiene sources for relief, instead of recognizing their enemy as the god of this world, who is trying to capture their minds. What the Christian needs at all times is to have on the whole armour of God, especially the helmet, which is "the hope of salvation" (I Thess. 5:8), to protect the mind against all doubts that Satan brings to us in this age of reasoning.

Three Questions

Nearly all worried Christian patients, after a long siege of satanic oppression, eventually present three questions, which depend upon the Christian's spiritual state and how much or how little time he spends in fellowship with the Lord. We shall consider first the question which is the all-important one for every individual to be able to answer in the affirmative with assurance: "Am I saved?"

Nervous Christian patients, if they are not spiritual, sooner or later reveal doubt in regard to their salvation. Satan knows that he cannot take away our salvation, which God gave us when we believed and accepted Christ as our Saviour; but he knows that he can cause us to doubt. He knows that when he has succeeded in getting us to doubt, he has scored the first victory in breaking our fellowship with God.

Christian, can you not see the subtle, psychological scheme of Satan in this? Worry and doubt, if we permit them, can put us into such bondage to self that all our thoughts will be on self. When all our thoughts are on self, we do not fellowship with God.

Then what shall the Christian do when doubt comes? Cast it on Jesus, moment by moment. "Casting all your care upon him; for he careth for you" (I Pet. 5:7). "Let not your heart be troubled" with such thoughts that come to mind—thoughts which try to hinder your sweet fellowship with Him so that you have no joy, no love for anyone, no peace, night or day. When doubt and conflict come, remember that God has not forsaken you, as so many of my patients want to believe. He is patiently waiting for you to look back to Calvary. Nervous Christian, look back to Calvary and renew your confidence in all that Jesus did for you there.

The second question involves a fear that is common to nervous Christian patients—the "why" of their suffering. They ask, "Is there some unconfessed sin in my life for which God is punishing me?"

When Christians are worried, they seem to forget their "first love" and their spiritual relationship with Christ. The fact that they have been redeemed and washed by the blood of the Lamb seems very remote. They forget that, as children of God through Christ, they have the right to "come boldly unto the throne of grace" at any time and ask forgiveness for sins committed. "If we confess our sins, he is faithful and just to forgive us our sins, and to cleanse us from all unrighteousness" (I John 1:9).

Satan, the accuser and liar, makes the patient believe that God put the suffering on him for past sins. He robs the patient of peace by reminding him of past sins which have been forgiven. To find a release from the accusation, the sufferer will attempt to make restitution for past deeds, or at least to perform certain religious duties, such as visiting the sick or sending Care packages to the needy of other countries, spending all his time doing things to merit forgiveness instead of just trusting the grace of God. If the matter of searching for unconfessed sin is carried too far, the patient may become overly scrupulous.

To the redeemed, God is no longer the wrathful God, but the loving God, who sees us with love because we are in Christ. God is not tempting us or accusing us of our past sins which have been forgiven and forgotten. Too many nervous Christian patients act as if God might forgive but never forget; but He says, "I, even I, am he that blotteth out thy transgressions for mine own sake, and will not remember thy sins" (Isa. 43:25).

The third question which invariably always comes up for consideration is this: "How long can you worry before you have a nervous breakdown? Am I having a nervous breakdown and don't know it?"

Spiritual Christians do not need much reassurance about their mental state. Christian psychotherapy helps them to understand that they have permitted themselves to become troubled about many things and that there is nothing wrong with the mind just because Satan tempts them with doubt and unwholesome thoughts. Christians who truly walk with God know what it means to be personally tested by the satanic forces which endeavor to break our fellowship with God by creating many doubts with regard to our faith and bringing them to the mind. These external spirit forces strive to control the thinking of Christians and revive the fleshly nature.

Nervous, carnal Christians have many questions dealing with the mind and mental hygiene.

Because of their worldly attitude, they have been reading extensively about mental problems and doing much self-analysis. They ask, "What books on psychology shall I read?" It is difficult for them to conceive of evil spirits influencing their thinking. Their reading matter, or mental food, is based on unregenerate man's psychological reasonings, which have no discernment for evil forces and influences. It is the carnal, worldly-minded Christians in our churches who take little by faith and absorb only what appeals to the reason. Carnal Christians who suffer with so-called nervous symptoms are spiritually confused.

Psychological Era

Surely we are living in the time of Daniel's prophecy: "The time of the end: many shall run to and fro, and knowledge shall be increased" (Dan. 12:4). "Ever learning, and never able to come to the knowledge of the truth" (II Tim. 3:7).

What is happening to the minds of men? Who is doing this? What evidence do we actually have that this time spoken of by Daniel is upon us?

"The prince of the power of the air," who is the god of this world, is blinding the minds of them who do not believe, so that the light of the gospel of Christ will not shine into their hearts. He does this by keeping the Bible on an intellectual level, leaving out everything that tends to suggest faith in Christ. He teaches about a Jesus, but not that Jesus is our Saviour and Lord. Finally, he has set

up church systems that deny Christ and His finished work on Calvary.

Satan's bloodless doctrines seem to attract and
soothe many anxious (nervous) patients who are
ardent apostles for their faith, but not of faith in
Christ. Most of these patients are blinded, as they
believe that they are saved by a new and better
religion.

Church members are carried away from Christ
by the hypnotic influence of this psychological era,
and many preachers as well as laymen have "itching ears." Paul prophesied, "And they shall turn
away their ears from the truth, and shall be turned
unto fables" (II Tim. 4:4)—man's reasonings devised to take truth out of the Bible.

Psychology is in the atmosphere. Christians
are being exposed to it through lectures, reading
material, radio, television, and even sermons. Some
time ago, after I had given a Christian message,
a minister spoke to me, saying, "Doctor, could you
not have given that to us a little more from the
psychological interpretation?"

Some ministers reluctantly give their sermons
a psychological flavor because they feel that is
what their audience desires; others freely substitute the reasonings of man for the scriptural truths.
Many Christians are searching the Scriptures, hoping to find Biblical passages to substantiate their
psychological views. Jesus Christ and the apostles
did not spend time expounding psychological theo-
ries of man; they preached the gospel. Psychology

appeals to the mind. The gospel appeals to the heart.

Satan is battling for the minds of men, using every psychological appeal that seems reasonable and acceptable to man. He knows that "there is a way that seemeth right unto a man" (Prov. 16:25), and he uses that "way." Christians should not blame the psychiatrist and the psychologist for this psychological trend, but rather consider the state of the heart that succumbs to the psychological appeal.

Remember, Jesus warns us that at the "end time" the evil forces will "seduce, if it were possible, even the elect" (Mark 13:22). Peter further admonishes us, "Beware lest ye also, being led away with the error of the wicked, fall from your own stedfastness" (II Pet. 3:17).

After a series of intermittent consultations, a young pastor made this revealing confession: "As I look back now to my purpose in coming to you, I really was not as worried about my thoughts as I was anxious to see how you counseled with patients. I wanted to get your technique of counseling and learn something that would give me prestige with my church and conference."

This patient's problem had been presented to me with the complaint, "I can't pray. My prayers hit the ceiling and bounce back down to me, even in church."

There certainly was cause for this man's inability to commune with God. He had a long emotional history in which his own confessions reveal that the imaginations of his heart were filled with sexual fantasies associated with women and that his mind could not concentrate on spiritual things because the thoughts and intents of his heart interfered.

He stumbled at the question, "Are you born again?" but tried to justify his religious works. There seemed to be no desire to give up his lustful fantasies, or to turn from his own psychological reasonings to the Word of God for guidance in counseling his parishioners.

Resisting the Spirit

Some of our college and university students try to find the answers to all problems by their own reasonings and by the psychological and atheistic philosophies of life. They "will" not to hear the Spirit say, "Come."

A certain young man who had resisted every attempt of the Holy Spirit to convict him, especially when he read the Bible, until love of sin and desire to do evil hardened his heart and dulled his mind, came for psychotherapy. He did not come to a psychiatrist because he desired a way out of his sinful ways, but because he realized that his mind was no longer entirely under his control and because of fears associated with his way of life.

He was in distress because his homosexual partner cooperated halfheartedly and finally denounced him and the whole affair as "filthy." The patient became frightened for fear he would be found out if he tried to make new contacts for himself. For the sake of good public appearance and to hide his queer reactions, he sought refuge in marriage—not that he desired a woman, but a woman would make an abode for him.

He sighed and yawned repeatedly during psychotherapy; and when some of the fear pressure subsided, he discontinued treatment because each consultation gave him much headache and irritability.

The tragedy of this man's spiritual condition and how it came about is briefly related in his own words: "In times past whenever I heard disparaging remarks about the Bible, I welcomed them. They helped to break down the power of the Bible. I imagined ridiculous things about the Bible. I had my own versions of Jonah and the whale, of Samson and Delilah. I have done this sort of thing until now when I try to think on the Bible, I cannot see through it, as it is all so ludicrous. I can concentrate on my studies and reason logically; but when I try to think about the Bible, it leaves me almost instantly. Even when I make an effort to concentrate on the Bible, I cannot hold the subject before me.

"I think I understand the psychological mechanism of this slipping away. The Bible was not pleasant; it was condemning. I see now that I pushed it away by letting my mind fantasy on sex. However, I never saw it, or got the full impact until you read Romans 1 to me. I evidently did not want to admit hearing God's call. Now sex is everything to me. I want to spend all my time looking at nude men, just as you read in Romans 1:28: 'And even as they did not like to retain God in their knowledge, God gave them over to a reprobate mind.'

"When you explain salvation, I want to argue every step of the way. Virgin and virgin birth, a man dying on the cross! Bah! The idea of a man being so self-righteous that he would become a martyr for a cause! He had no cause! There is no hell! More people believe there is no hell than there are people who believe there is a hell."

Satan had this patient's mind always channeled open for lustful thoughts; any other trend of thinking was boredom to him. "I seem to have a desire to cooperate with you, but I suddenly get such a tired, bored feeling." He was bound by Satan, "taken captive by him at his will," to do the will of the adversary.

During psychotherapy, because of his fear, he tried to read the Gospel of John while the radio was on. But he was not convicted to repentance in his heart.

The Battle Is Real

Christian, Satan knows that the "end time" is upon us. He knows that his doom is about to be eternally sealed, and he is desperate in his battle for the minds of men. Your only defense against him is the "whole armour of God," who promises us that if we take "the shield of faith," we "shall be able to quench all the fiery darts of the wicked" (Eph. 6:16).

Do not be overcome by Satan. Do not let him confuse your mind until it is entirely taken up with meditating on your worries, anxieties, and fears. Your mind is under the blood. You have been purchased with a price, which is the precious blood of Christ, and your whole being—mind, body, and soul—is under the blood.

Satan is real. There is a Devil. If I had not known this before, it would most certainly have been revealed to me through the mental torture and the soul anguish poured forth from the hearts of my patients.

Perhaps more evil imaginations are revealed in the psychiatrist's consultation room than in any other place. But the psychiatrist does not know the half, because the half has never been told. "The heart is deceitful above all things, and desperately wicked: who can know it?" (Jer. 17:9). ONLY GOD!

7

SOUL SUFFERING IN SICKNESS

The onset of the spiritual suffering begins the moment the individual turns from God's guidance. Adam realized this instantly when he disobeyed God. As the Christian continues on his course outside God's guiding eye, the guilt in the soul builds up in intensity, causing a confused mind and eventually a sick body. When the soul suffers, the body and the mind suffer with it. When the body suffers, the mind and the soul suffer with it. "And whether one member suffer, all the members suffer with it" (I Cor. 12:26).

Repressed worries are really not repressed and forgotten, as we would like to believe. They are never stationary, but grow and become more complex as we add more cares and finally reach the place where we are ensnared and all taken up with self-concern.

When the so-called nervous Christian patient finds himself slipping into such a mess, God does not expect him to take the same course as the unsaved, who divert their thoughts with things of the world when worried. God has something better for us Christians. We are His redeemed, blood-bought children, very precious in His sight.

He did not redeem us in order that we might adjust to this world and wait until we die physically to enter into His glory. He gave us the Holy Spirit as a Comforter, Instructor, and Guide through this wilderness journey. But many Christians are slow and reluctant to follow the leading of this Pilot. Instead they stumble along in their own way and become weary, fretful, and discouraged. Their new nature has fitted them for heaven, but they are trying to indulge in former lusts. The Holy Spirit convicts them that they are guilty.

Healing for Nervous Christians

There is no doubt in the mind of the Christian that God can and does heal in our times. He heals in many miraculous ways today, using human instruments as His agents. He is "the same yesterday, and today, and for ever" (Heb. 13:8).

The "nervous" Christian, by his very nature of being anxious, is susceptible to all kinds of doctrines of healing that offer hope for relief. In his anxious state he is not able to "discern the spirits" and is carried away with various spurious doctrines. He believes that he should try them because they claim a basic truth from the Bible.

Not all who seek such healing are healed. In fact, many are left confused, bitter, discouraged, and embarrassed to face their Christian friends, fearing that they will accuse them of a hidden, unconfessed sin or lack of faith. Because of this prevailing attitude, some nervous Christian patients would feel condemned if they should seek relief for emotional and physical suffering from scientific medical sources.

Apparently they are not conscious of the Biblical fact that one of the Gospel writers, Doctor Luke, was a physician, and that Paul had Doctor Luke with him on his missionary journeys as his personal physician.

We read that Paul sought divine healing for himself, but God deemed it wiser to leave him with a "thorn in the flesh" to keep him humble. Surely if healing depended on faith and a close walk with God, Paul would have been healed.

We read also that Paul was used of God to heal many sufferers while on his missionary journeys. Yet God did not choose to heal all of Paul's patients; for Paul writes, "Trophimus have I left at Miletum sick" (II Tim. 4:20).

Furthermore, if there was to be no sickness and suffering, there would necessarily, of course, be no death of the body.

Today God answers the prayers of his saints for the healing of the sick when He deems it best, according to His divine plan and will. He puts His approval and blessing on human agents (physicians and surgeons) to relieve man's suffering. Medical men frequently attest to the fact that the patients seemed hopeless, but for some reason beyond man's power they recovered after surgery patched up a wrecked physical body. Likewise, medicine taken for relief of bodily suffering and fatigue has its useful place; even sedatives are necessary for both Christians and non-Christians to help them through a crisis.

The fear that their friends will think they do not have faith in the Lord Jesus if they seek medical help has caused many nervous Christian patients to delay seeking help for themselves until they have been overtaken with a debilitating chronic illness, not only causing much needless suffering, but an early death, as well as economic distress for their families.

Miserable Comforters

Truly, soul suffering is harder to endure than any other form of suffering, because no one but the Great Physician can examine the soul and recognize the germ that started the whole suffering complex, which eventually comes to the surface as mind and body suffering. Too often zealous people add suffering to suffering when they mimic Job's comforters. Job said of them, because they saw his suffering as they wanted to see it, "Ye are all physicians of no value" (Job 13:4), and "Miserable comforters are ye all" (Job 16:2).

Likewise, many patients today must endure "religious" exhortations, such as, "You must have some unconfessed sin." . . . "Pray about it." . . . "You lack faith in God."

There may be no hidden sin to confess. The patient may be living day by day according to God's promise: "If we confess our sins, he is faithful and just to forgive us our sins, and to cleanse us from all unrighteousness" (I John 1:9).

Furthermore, to urge the suffering patients to look for hidden sins makes them more introspective and limits their thinking more and more to nar-

rowed self. Then they become frightened and say
to themselves, "I believe I am losing my mind." All
of this naturally makes the patient a fit subject
for a psychiatrist.

One wonders if self-appointed advisers ever
consider that they might be adding to the patient's
heartache and suffering!

Suffering Not for Sin

The question is this: What is God's will, or
plan, in the individual's life? Is the suffering a
result of his own indulgence, his own way of life;
or is God letting some of his saints go through the
furnace of affliction for a refining process, so that
they will come forth as vessels that will glorify
God? We have the story of the man who was born
blind, suffering that inconvenience until he met
Jesus. Our Lord tells us that this was not because
of the man's sin, but that the healing, and later the
testimony of the sufferer, would glorify God.

Many Christians cannot accept their suffering
as graciously as Paul, who finally came up with
the words of grace, "Most gladly therefore will I
rather glorify in my infirmities, that the power of
Christ may rest upon me" (II Cor. 12:9).

We Christians dare not be critical of the suffering of other Christians. How can we judge?
After all, we cannot read God's mind, and we are
only measuring the other saint's suffering from
our position. God calls each saint for a special
ministry: "But the manifestation of the Spirit is
given to every man to profit withal. For to one is

given by the Spirit the word of wisdom; to another the word of knowledge by the same Spirit" (I Cor. 12:7,8).

It is apparent in observing the suffering of some saints that God calls and gives to each according to measure. Not all saints will endure alike, and God knows who will trust Him and be led by Him. That is why some saints are used mightily of God, whereas many others placed in the same position would fold up and be a discredit to His holy Name.

God Is So Far Away

Nervous patients who have been suffering for a long time say, "God is so far away. He does not hear my prayers. He has forsaken me and is punishing me for some of my past sins."

Let us go back again to the preceding paragraphs and note the insidious onset of the spiritual disease. They were careless toward God and walked away from Him, turning their heart's desire to the things of the world. God did not forsake them. He is ever faithful, but they forsook God. If God seems far away from us, it only signifies how far we have walked from Him.

God has given us a definite plan of spiritual hygiene by which we can avoid being overtaken by emotional and nervous symptoms.

Self-Judgment—Key to Spiritual Health

When the child of God senses guilt, he should take this sign as a symptom that all is not well in the spiritual sense, consider it as a warning, and apply it in the same light as a person uses a thermometer to gauge the temperature of the physical body.

Self-judgment is one of the most healthful exercises that a Christian can rely upon to keep himself in excellent spiritual health. Self-judgment is present in every born-again Christian. But its effectiveness as a preventive guide depends upon how closely the Christian walks with God; whether he will turn to God immediately, or whether he chooses to go his own way and bring upon himself fear, anxiety, mental confusion, and bodily suffering.

There is no need for guilt to remain on the conscience. When the child of God senses guilt and fear, the Holy Spirit is bidding him to come boldly to the throne of grace and repent, confess, and ask forgiveness. He has promised that "if we confess our sin, he is faithful and just to forgive us our sins, and to cleanse us from all unrighteousness" (I John 1:9).

When we realize that we can stand in His presence as if we had never sinned, the guilt is gone. The very fact that we do not confess at the first signs of guilt shows that we really are reluctant to yield ourselves to Him. There is something in our self-nature that we desire to retain and enjoy; for if we were really yielded, we would not hesitate, but would rely on Him and His grace.

It is the flesh lusting "against the Spirit" that makes us unhappy, concerned, anxious, and worried. All the soul anguish and mental torment, and months and years of nervousness, could be avoided if we would go to Him as soon as we realize that we are too absorbed with cares and anxiety concerning things in this world that tend to make us forget that we are looking for Him, to be joined to Him. Jesus said, "But seek ye first the kingdom of God, and his righteousness; and all these things shall be added unto you" (Matt. 6:33).

Nervous Christians and Works

The nervous Christian patient, being sensitive to what goes on about him, must be on his guard. The spirit of anxiety and insecurity which permeates the atmosphere of the "worldly" is contagiously affecting the Christians until they too are ruining and exhausting their bodies with over-much activity. However, they have deceived themselves into believing that they should be busy about the Lord's business with too many church activities and the innumerable worthy religious organizations. They do not realize that the "prince of this world" has deceived them over much worthy Christian activity until they forget to find time to commune with the Lord.

Three missionaries, sent home recently from their fields of service, each with a nervous breakdown, complained that they had so many duties to look after on the field that there was no time for quiet meditation and Bible study.

Many ministers of our churches have the same complaint. These activities, even though they are worthy, should not drive us until we are too fatigued bodily and emotionally to spend time with the Lord.

The Lord Jesus knew that His disciples needed to rest from their labors (rest in Him) and that they needed to receive strength through fellowship with Him. He said to them, "Come ye yourselves apart into a desert place, and rest a while" (Mark 6:31).

"Who Healeth All Thy Diseases"

Psalm 103:3 is often forced out of context. Let not the Christian expect God to heal him when he is defying God's natural laws of health, whether it be immoral habits, lustful appetites of the flesh, or just plain gluttony in eating. If one willfully abuses his body, the temple of the soul, in which dwells the Spirit of God, "him shall God destroy" (I Cor. 3:16,17).

The Christian cannot defile his body and then expect to offer his body as "a living sacrifice." We cannot violate God's laws of health and get by. When we violate His rules of health, we will suffer. Just because suffering and punishment are not dealt out immediately when we defy the rules of health does not imply that we are getting by.

For instance, the man who smokes just a little every day is taking into his system a deadly poison —nicotine. Be it ever so small, it is very toxic to many organs of the body which may eventually cause sudden death by heart attack or cancer of the respiratory system. He is not ignorant and is therefore without excuse, for he is deliberately taking poison into his body, defiling the "temple of God."

It seems a bit strange that reason and logic would not stop even the worldly-minded from damaging his body. But when a Christian indulges in such passions, it demonstrates his bondage to the old desires and the fact that Christ does not have first place in his life. The sin is not in the tobacco, but in the heart of the man who endeavors to release his emotional tension without turning to God. In like manner, alcohol is not the sin; but the man with a sinful heart takes it in order to satisfy the evil desires of his heart.

The Christian who turns his back on God and resorts to alcoholic drinks to soothe his emotions and to produce exhilarant feelings in place of turning to the joy of Christ within knows the consequences from the beginning.

His relatives and friends pray "without ceasing" that God will take away his desire for liquor, but their prayers go unanswered, because the cause for the desire is still in the man's heart. They should pray, rather, that the Lord will bring conviction upon him so that he will cry out for deliverance of the sin in his heart.

God does not promise to heal man of the outward manifestations of disease which have been brought on by sinful emotions and desires, until he has repented in the heart. The prerequisite of deliverance is repentance. Jesus often said to those whom He healed, "Thy sins be forgiven thee." The healing of the disease follows the cleansing of the heart.

Overeating

Trying to satisfy anxiety by eating leads to obesity. Everybody knows the potential danger of being overweight. Food is not poisonous; yet when it is taken to excess, the body is poisoned from its effect. Thus the man suffering emotionally in his soul from anxiety and insecurity eats more or less continually to appease that tension. The sick soul in this case makes the body suffer from the effects of obesity, which in turn may have a deleterious effect on the body, causing physical disease, and may shorten man's span of life.

We, as Christians, should not permit our emotions to lead us into habits of overindulgence which cause suffering. The Christian is not supposed to appease his anxieties by unwholesome habits, for the Word of God says, "Be careful (anxious) for nothing; but in every thing by prayer and supplication with thanksgiving let your requests be made known unto God" (Phil. 4:6).

THE CHRISTIAN'S WARFARE

by Theodore H. Epp

The child of God is engaged in a spiritual warfare. Paul wrote, "We wrestle not against flesh and blood, but against principalities, against powers, against the rulers of the darkness of this world, against spiritual wickedness in high places" (Eph. 6:12). But let it be clearly understood at the outset that believers are on the winning side. In Christ Jesus we are more than conquerors (Rom. 8:37). Our spiritual resources are the Lord himself and the power of His might (Eph. 6:10). In Christ Jesus we can have victory at all times. There is no need of succumbing to any satanic wiles, fiery darts, or wicked devices.

As you read the New Testament, you cannot fail to note that Christians are often warned against the wiles of the Devil. Our Saviour spoke about them to His disciples. Paul and Peter sound strong warnings concerning the evil one and his subtle traps. In each case the warning is to the saved, not the unsaved. It is God's children who are to put on the whole armour of God. It is they who are to be strong in the Lord. Paul said that "we" wrestle against principalities and powers. Knowing now the identity of our foes, and confident of victory in this fight, let us take a closer look at how Satan, through his evil forces, seeks to gain control of the believer and dominate his life.

There are some who think that all that is needed in this warfare is to know God, but to pay no attention to the enemy. That is one of Satan's cleverest devices. Much of his success lies in the fact that he so cleverly hides his identity that men do not suspect his evil presence or his purposes. But I want you to see from the Bible the methods which Satan employs to both oppress and obsess whomever he can among God's people.

Satanic Oppression

Peter, in speaking to the household of Cornelius concerning Jesus, said, "God anointed Jesus of Nazareth with the Holy Ghost and with power: who went about doing good, and healing all that were oppressed of the devil" (Acts 10:38). The word "oppress" is significant. It means "to exercise control over" or "to tyrannize." The indication is clear that such oppression is not from within, but from without, and comes from satanic forces.

One of the things they do is put the saints under great mental and emotional pressure. You hear much about this condition these days, but I assure you that a Christian does not have to live under such pressure. He can be free from it even though it is all around him. That is why we are told in Ephesians 6 to be strong *in the power of His might,* and to put on the whole armour of God.

A striking passage with regard to the battle for control of the believer's mind is II Corinthians

10:3-5, where we read: "For though we walk in the flesh, we do not war after the flesh: (For the weapons of our warfare are not carnal, but mighty through God to the pulling down of strong holds;) Casting down imaginations, and every high thing that exalteth itself against the knowledge of God, *and bringing into captivity every thought* to the obedience of Christ." Why would God say this if Satan, through his evil forces, were not constantly attacking the hearts and minds of believers in order to put them under pressure? It may be pressure of work, or of the home, or of the church. It could be pressure for almost any reason. By not realizing the real source of our trouble, we may blame other people, or perhaps some accident that we have had; but many times these things are what Satan uses to put us under strain.

Some Examples of Satanic Pressure

Not long ago we received a very informative letter along this line from a missionary with whom we have had some enjoyable fellowship. His communication showed that he was having victory over satanic forces out there in a heathen land. He told, for example, how he had lost his passport, and he added, "It could have gotten me very vexed, for what Satan wanted was to spoil the image of Christ in me. He wasn't concerned about my passport. I acknowledged that it was Satan, and I took the victory stand against him; and then I found my passport." He named three or four other things that had happened to him recently in which he was able to discern that Satan was trying to oppress him. With regard to them he said, "I found the victory in Christ every time, and then the other things straightened out, too."

We can gain victory over Satan, who already is a defeated foe (Heb. 2:14; Col. 2:15), any time we will claim it in the Name of Jesus. We must oppose Satan directly in the Name of Jesus and claim the power of the blood of Christ as our protection.

For a number of years I felt these pressures. At times, in order to find relief, I got into my car and drove out into the country to have a talk with God, and eventually the depression left me. Then one day I realized that such pressure could be coming from Satan. I knew the way of victory in the Word and took it. It has not been necessary for me to go into the country for the past year or two to get rid of this heart and mind pressure, because I found the way of victory. God gave me discernment to see that satanic forces were bringing this depression upon my mind in an effort to control me.

Satanic Obsession

After Satan has scored success in oppressing the Christian, he takes up the second phase of his work, which is obsession. This work is brought to our attention in such a passage as Luke 6:18, where we read how sick people were brought to Jesus: "And they that were vexed with unclean spirits: and they were healed." The word "vexed" is the one to note here. We find it again in Acts 5:16: "There came also a multitude . . . bringing sick folks, and them which were vexed with unclean spirits." "To vex" comes from a Greek word meaning "to obsess," "to harass," "to mob," or "to riot." It speaks of a vicious attack made by demons upon a person.

An illustration from Matthew 12:44 will help make this clear, even though an unsaved person is apparently referred to here. When a demon is driven out of a person, the demon seeks another abode but finds none. Then he returns to the person whom he originally controlled and finds that this one is not possessed by the Holy Spirit, but is merely reformed (empty). Then the demon calls in seven others to help him harass this person. They come like a flood, and the first thing they will attack is the mind.

Satan Attacks Christians' Minds

Satanic forces will attack the minds of Christians also. They suggest doubts to us, especially doubts concerning the goodness of God. Instead of having the mind of God and the mind of Christ, we suddenly begin to think the thoughts suggested by one of the demons. A mind obsessed by Satan thinks evil of God. In order to avoid this, we are told, "Let this mind be in you, which was also in Christ Jesus" (Phil. 2:5).

That the mental powers of a believer may be affected by demons is indicated in II Corinthians 10:4,5, a passage to which we have already referred. But read again those startling statements which show that we have God-given weapons for the "pulling down of strong holds; casting down imaginations, and every high thing that exalteth itself against the knowledge of God." Do you understand? It is not just the unsaved, but also the saved who can have their minds obsessed by evil ideas about God.

Some of Satan's Methods

See now some of the ways in which these demon powers try to harass Christians. Possibly the most common method is by worry. Instead of having the peace of God, which passes all understanding, and which would keep our emotions in proper balance and our minds thinking correctly, we worry.

Someone wrote to me recently, "You're not the only one who has worries. I have worries, too." I thank God that He has helped me so that if I have any worries, I am not aware of them. Instead of worries I have His peace, which expels worries. Satan's trick, however, is to capitalize on worry and through that to take control of the believer's mind.

Another of Satan's devices is to get us to fret over some situation in life instead of being content. Paul, in Philippians 4:11, said, "I have learned, in whatsover state I am . . . to be content." In other words, there had been times when he fretted, but he learned to overcome Satan's power in the strength of the Lord.

Then there is a complaining spirit to which some people succumb. There are those who always see the dark side of things. Of course, this is carried to greater excess with some than with others, but Satan will foster that in our hearts if he can thereby get control of our minds.

"Oh, it's my nature," is the explanation which Christians often give when confronted with this truth. We agree, but we would add that it is Satan working through their nature. Do not at any time excuse yourself on the basis of your nature. When Jesus Christ died, the old nature was crucified with Him. In your daily experience you are to keep it on the cross, and this you can do with the help of the Lord. Then live in the nature of our Lord.

Vain imagination is another of Satan's tools. He likes to get us to imagining that somebody hates us. I talked to an unsaved woman not too long ago who imagined that even God hated her. Satan was certainly obsessing her mind. But there are Christians who actually feel that way. That is a satanic imagination.

Another of Satan's tricks today is to cause God's people to have evil thoughts about others. A common method is to get us to attribute wrong motives to their actions. This, too, is giving way to vain imaginations.

Then there are impure thoughts, which seem to run riot at times. Someone knocked at our door one night. The time was about 1:00 a.m. I went to see who was there and found that it was a man whom I knew. As he stood there, I saw that his eyes were staring, and his face was white with fear.

I invited him in, and he said, "You've got to help me, Brother Epp! You've got to help me!"

He then began to pour out in vile language the most impure thoughts I have heard since I was saved. Immediately I said to him, "Man, do you know what's happened to you? Satan has taken possession of your mind."

He answered, "I know it."

We prayed. God gave the victory. The man was released. The stare left his eyes. The color returned to his face. He got up and said, "Thank you, Brother Epp. That's all I needed."

That was Satan at work. The case was an extreme one, I grant you. Many of you have not gone that far, but you have gotten started with impure thoughts. They come through Satan's vexing the mind.

We have only touched on these matters, and the following is but a partial list, some of which we have already discussed: worry, fretting, complaining, vain imaginations, evil thoughts, impure thoughts, anger, harshness, suspicion, fanaticism, irritableness, critical spirit, spirit of revenge, fear, grief, contention, impatience, sensitiveness, pride, frustration, heresy, conceit, jealousy, and many others.

The Way of Victory

Let me remind you of what I said at the beginning of this study. In Christ we have a Saviour who provides complete victory over Satan and all his evil devices. You can resist Satan and be an overcomer at all times. First, recognize that he is already a defeated foe (Heb. 2:14; Col. 2:15). That is very important. Then recognize the fact that God has transferred you into Christ's kingdom, according to Colossians 1:13: "Who hath delivered us from the power of darkness, and hath translated us into the kingdom of his dear Son." For these reasons and more, Satan cannot lord it over you against your will.

In Ephesians 6, which is a message to God's people, we are instructed to put on every piece of the armour of God. Let us do just that. Claim the power of the blood. Claim the power of the Word. Bind Satan by a positive stand against him in the Name of Jesus, and say, "I am under the blood, Satan. Be gone!"

THE ESSENTIAL THING IS FAITH. "Fight the good fight of faith" (I Tim. 6:12). Remember these facts: (1) Satan has been overpowered. (2) Satan is a defeated foe. (3) We must withstand him directly with this knowledge. Then, having complete faith in the Word and in the power of Christ's Name, we stand victors. But we must believe these things, or else Satan will gain the advantage over us because of our lack of faith.

Be constantly on the alert. Be prepared daily to resist Satan by feeding upon the Word and by continually being filled with the Holy Spirit. Then Satan will not be able to touch you in any way whatsoever.